CITYSPOTS
VERONA

Barbara Radcl
Stillman Roge

Thomas Cook

Written by Barbara Radcliffe Rogers
Original photography by Stillman Rogers
Front cover photography courtesy of AM Corporation/Alamy Images
Series design based on an original concept by Studio 183 Limited

Produced by Cambridge Publishing Management Limited
Project Editor: Penny Isaac
Layout: Julie Crane
Maps: PC Graphics
Transport map: © Communicarta Limited

Published by Thomas Cook Publishing
A division of Thomas Cook Tour Operations Limited
Company Registration No. 1450464 England
PO Box 227, Unit 18, Coningsby Road
Peterborough PE3 8SB, United Kingdom
email: books@thomascook.com
www.thomascookpublishing.com
+ 44 (0) 1733 416477

ISBN-13: 978-1-84157-649-7
ISBN-10: 1-84157-649-2

First edition © 2006 Thomas Cook Publishing
Text © 2006 Thomas Cook Publishing
Maps © 2006 Thomas Cook Publishing
Series/Project Editor: Kelly Anne Pipes
Production/DTP: Steven Collins

Printed and bound in Spain by GraphyCems

CONTENTS

INTRODUCING VERONA

Introduction 6
When to go.....................................8
The Verona opera 12
History..14
Lifestyle..16
Culture 18

MAKING THE MOST OF VERONA

Shopping...22
Eating & drinking 24
Entertainment & nightlife......28
Sport & relaxation 30
Accommodation 32
The best of Verona 38
Something for nothing 42
When it rains................................44
On arrival.......................................46

THE CITY OF VERONA

The Old Centre 56
The Arena & West.......................78

OUT OF TOWN TRIPS

Around Verona.............................94
Vicenza 106
Lake Garda 122

PRACTICAL INFORMATION

Directory.......................................140
Useful phrases 152
Emergencies 154

INDEX...158

MAP LIST

Verona city map 48
Verona transport map..............52
Old Centre.....................................57
The Arena & West 79
Around Verona 95
Vicenza 107
Lake Garda 123

SYMBOLS & ABBREVIATIONS

The following symbols are used throughout this book:

ⓐ address ☎ telephone ⓕ fax ⓔ email ⓦ website address
🕐 opening times Ⓝ public transport connections ❶ important

The following symbols are used on the maps:

ℹ️ information office		○	city
✈️ airport		○	large town
➕ hospital		○	small town
🚓 police station		═	motorway
🚌 bus station		▬	main road
🚆 train station		▬	minor road
✝️ cathedral		—	railway
❶ numbers denote featured cafés & restaurants			

Hotels and restaurants are graded by approximate price as follows:
£ budget **££** mid-range **£££** expensive

◑ *Castel San Pietro and the Roman theatre*

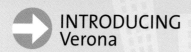

INTRODUCING
Verona

Introduction

Shakespeare never set foot in Verona, but he gave it a widespread –
although curious – claim to immortality as the home of the entirely
fictional Juliet. The legend continues to grow, bringing tourists from
all over the world to the beautiful old walled city. Brought here in
search of a myth, these tourists cannot help falling under the city's
very real spell. The old streets, elegant and intimate squares, fine
Renaissance palaces, medieval castle, Roman remains and art – not
to mention the warm-hearted and friendly people – give the city
as romantic an appeal in real life as Shakespeare's powerful play
did in fiction.

The old city centre, called the *centro storico* (historic centre),
is still the heart of Veronese life, just as it was when Romans
shopped in its markets, drank wine in its taverns and argued in
the forum. The clothes and hairstyles may be different, but these
same rhythms of life continue in modern Verona, and in much
the same places.

Verona is a lively city, filled with students and with young
tourists that keep its nightlife hip. It's no Milan, but nor does it have
Milan's prices or its rigid 'Armani-only' mindset. In the summer, the
action moves to Lake Garda, to the small towns along the eastern
shore – Bardolino, Garda and Lazise – and to the larger Decenzano di
Garda. Especially at weekends, these towns are filled with people of
all ages, and the younger ones keep clubs, pubs and lakeside bars
open until late.

Few places in Italy have managed to keep the most appealing of
their historic relics without becoming a static museum of some far-
off time. Here, though, there is the best-preserved Roman Arena in
Italy – which is still in use for everything from grand opera to rock

concerts – as well as other outstanding Roman, medieval and Renaissance sites. These both act as a backdrop and play an active role in the city. Here Gucci, grand opera and gladiators join hip-hop, Shakespeare's Juliet and mobile phones in a mix so pleasantly blended that it's hard to draw the line between past and present.

🔺 *Past and present mingle in this lively city*

When to go

SEASONS & CLIMATE

Of all the things Verona has to brag about, the weather isn't one of them. Winter is a sulky grey stretch that seems to last from November to March. From April to October, you can still find stretches of grey weather, along with frequent showers, but you will also find beautiful blue-sky days, balmy and pleasant with refreshing evenings. The city in July and August can be stiflingly hot and this is a good time to join the locals, who flee to breezy Lake Garda for evenings, weekends and most of the month of August. However, unlike most Italian cities, Verona doesn't shut down altogether during August, because that's the height of the opera festival, when the Arena hosts 15,000 opera-goers four evenings a week.

ANNUAL EVENTS

January

Rogo del Pan e Vin Starting on about 5 January, these are bonfires held throughout the northern part of Italy, whether it is to welcome the New Year or drive out the evil spirits of the past year – nobody's sure.

February

Carnevale di Verona Although it begins officially on 6 January, most of the excitement is in February. ⓐ Ducato di S. Stefano Carnevale Benefico, Via San Giovanni in Valle, 13/c, Verona. ⓦ www.ducatosantostefano.it

March
Vinitaly Wine and Food Show Late March to early April. One of the biggest wine shows in Italy. Accommodation may be hard to find.
🅰 Ente Autonomo Fiere di Verona, Viale del Lavoro 8, Verona
🕿 045 829 8111 🌐 www.vinitaly.com

April
Liberation Day 25 April. Celebrated throughout Italy, in Verona it is marked in and around Piazza Brà.
Mondadori Junior Festival Children's activities all over town, from a play-park inside the Arselale grounds to ravioli-making on Piazza Brà.
Montecchio Medievale Late April and early May. Centred on the two castles above the city, the festival includes medieval pageantry and the Romeo and Juliet story. 🅰 Ufficio Turismo e Spettccolo
🕿 044 470 5721 🕿 044 469 4888

May
Le Piazze dei Sapori Sample the flavours of Italy at this great food-fest in the middle of Piazza Brà. 🅰 Confesercenti Verona 🕿 045 862 4011 🌐 www.lepiazzedeisapori.com

CARNEVALE DI VERONA
The festivities begin on Epiphany (6 January) with the investiture of the Duca de la Pignata (Duke of the Pot) and from then until the end of February, Verona is home to a fantastic Carnevale that envelops the entire city in colourful pageantry and fun. The event culminates in late February with a parade and presentation of masks, dancing, the distribution of traditional minestrone, wine and chocolate, and a final celebratory dinner.

Festa Medioevale del Vino Bianco Soave (Soave Medieval Wine Festival). Medieval costumes are everywhere, but the wine and goodies are contemporary. Ⓦ www.comunesoave.it

June

Arena di Verona Opera June to August. Scheduled opera performances take place in the 2,000-year-old Arena. Ⓐ Piazza Brà Ⓦ www.arena.it

Festival Shakespeariano A long-running Shakespeare festival where the works of the bard are performed in the city's 2,000-year-old Teatro Romano, in English with Italian subtitles. Ⓐ Comune di Verona Ⓣ 045 806 6485, 045 806 6488 Ⓦ www.estateteatraleveronese.it

July

Verona Vinorum A grand exposition of the finest Veronese wines, from Soave to the Valpolicellas. Ⓐ Palazzo Gran Guardia on Piazza Brà Ⓦ www.veronavinorum.it

August

Ferragosto 15 August. The Feast of the Assumption is celebrated throughout the region with a public holiday and various festivals.

Festa dell'apicoltura e del Miele della Lessinia Includes demonstrations and sales of honey products, plus general carnival fun. Ⓐ Piazza della Chiesa, Bosco Chiesanouva Ⓣ 045 705 0088.

September

Juliet's Birthday 16 September. An entirely fictitious excuse for Renaissance revelry and romantic doings throughout Verona.

Fiera dell'Uva (Grape Festival) Held in Soave at the beginning of the harvest in mid-September. ⓦ www.veronavinorum.it

Cura dell'Uva (Grape Cure Festival) Celebrates the produce of the Bardolino region from mid-September to mid-October.

October

Maratona di Verona Verona's marathon is run almost entirely within the old city. ➋ Corte Pancaldo 70 ☎ 045 818 3847 🖷 045 818 3888 ⓦ www.maratonadiverona.it

November

Tutti i Santi (All Saints' Day) 1 November is a public holiday throughout the region.

December

Festa del Immacolata Concezione 8 December. A religious festival and a public holiday.

Festa di Santa Lucia Mid-December. Stalls of goodies line Piazza Brà as everyone awaits the arrival of Santa Lucia with her crown of candles.

PUBLIC HOLIDAYS

New Year's Day 1 January	**All Saints' Day** (*Tutti i Santi*) 1 November
Epiphany 6 January	
Easter Monday March/April	**Feast of the Immaculate Conception** (*Immacolata Concezione*) 7–8 December
Liberation Day 25 April	
Labour Day 1 May	
Republic Day 2 June	
Feast of the Assumption (*Ferragosto*) 15 August	**Christmas Day** 25 December

The Verona opera

In August 1913 an audience assembled in Verona's 1st-century Roman Arena to hear a memorial performance of *Aida*. The spectacular was such a success that audiences have come in the summer ever since to hear some of the world's finest artists and musicians perform opera and ballet.

The sheer size of the place is impressive. The stage floor is the largest in Europe at approximately 44 m (145 ft) by 26 m (86 ft). The Arena holds up to 20,000 people. Seating around the inside is on 45 rows – made of marble, so bring something soft to sit on. Performances don't begin until the sky is dark, and the entire surrounding area becomes part of the stage. The grand scale of the arena also allows the use of unusual stage props as well.

During one performance of *Aida*, a flowing River Nile was built so that Aida could be rowed to her meeting with Radames.

Opera is the national music of Italy, and audiences span all ages. Here it's regarded as popular entertainment and is not something reserved only for highbrow audiences.

Opera season brings crowds to Verona from June to August. Hotel rooms are at a premium, so early booking is essential. Plan to park your car and walk into town and be sure to make reservations for pre- and post-opera dining.

Programme and tickets: ⓐ Fondazione Arena di Verona, Piazza Brà 28 ⓣ 045 800 5151 ⓦ www.arena.it

🔽 *Setting for a spectacular: the massive Roman Arena*

History

Location shaped Verona's history. Situated at the outlet of the Brenner Pass, the major gateway from northern Europe, it stands at the base of the Dolomite Mountains and on the northern edge of the fertile Po valley; it was certain to be a place where cultures met and clashed.

In about 200 BC, early hunter-gatherers living in the caves of Valpolicella were overcome by the Cenomani, a Gallic-Celtic tribe allied to the Romans. As Rome gathered strength and pushed its empire northwards, it moved across the lands of the Etruscans and on into the foothills of the Dolomiti, establishing a colony at Verona in 89 BC. The strategic position of the city was ideal, and it grew wealthy and important. By the 1st century AD it was a major Roman city.

As the Roman empire crumbled and northern tribes invaded, Verona was right in their path. The Ostrogoths arrived in 489 under King Theodoric, who promptly set up shop in a castle overlooking the city. Invading Lombards followed, before Charlemagne arrived in 774. He left his son Pepin in charge; legend has him buried under the tower of San Zeno.

In 1260 control of the city fell to Mastino I della Scala, a happy turn for the Veronese, who prospered under his family for several generations. Much that you see today was built by this powerful medieval family. The Visconti, from Milan, displaced them briefly before the Venetian Empire took charge in 1405.

Venice remained in control until it surrendered its empire to Napoleon in 1796. As Napoleon's fortunes turned, Verona was ceded to Austria; in spite of the Italian independence movement, Austria retained tight control over the entire region through the

Risorgimento, until the Battle of Solferino in 1859. In 1866 Verona became a part of the new united Italy.

As an ally of England and the United States in World War I, Verona and the nearby mountain region suffered heavy attacks from Austrian armies. In World War II, after Italy abandoned its alliance with the Nazis, the Italian dictator, Benito Mussolini, escaped to Salò on Lake Garda. Here the Germans established the puppet 'Salò Republic' for him.

Thousands of Veronese and other northern Italians joined Resistance movements against the Germans, many paying with their lives (memorial plaques on buildings show where Resistance members were shot or hanged by the Nazis). As the German forces withdrew in 1945, all the bridges in Verona – even the historic ones of no strategic value – were blown up.

Although heavily damaged during World War II, Verona pulled together and rebuilt – so skilfully that the Roman and medieval bridges show no signs of having been destroyed. Today the city is important to the Italian economy as a major agricultural and manufacturing centre.

Lifestyle

Although never considered one of Italy's avant-garde cities in the way Turin or Milan are, Verona is far from stodgy. That makes it a comfortable city for everyone, and perhaps the thing that will strike you first is the mix of ages nearly everywhere. The ladies-who-lunch, Versace-clad Italo-yuppies, drowsy elderly men and college students in their carefully ripped jeans are likely to frequent the same corner bar ... and smile and nod at each other as they arrive.

Although it might not have been the most egalitarian place in the past, Verona in the 21st century is a pretty democratic place, with room for all tastes, all types and all opinions (though the latter may be loudly argued through just before elections). It's always been a hard-working and largely working-class city, despite the Venetian palaces and the elegant art nouveau villas across the river.

And what does this mean for the tourist? That he or she will be accepted, tolerated, welcomed, helped or left alone in pretty much the same proportions as they might be at home.

Despite its uncertain weather (or maybe because of it), Verona is an outdoor city, and on a nice evening or weekend afternoon it seems as though 75 per cent of the population is in Piazza Brà. The cafés and park benches are filled to capacity, people stroll or stand around chatting, and even the steps of the two grand palaces facing the square are turned into impromptu seating.

● *The ever-busy Piazza Brà*

Culture

Although they are not pretentious about it, culture plays a big part in Veronese life. Wealthy patrons have always supported the city's artists, as a look inside the many churches will demonstrate. The big 'outsider' names are represented – you'll see a Titian painting in the Duomo and a Tintoretto in San Giorgio in Braida – but much of the decoration was commissioned from locals who were then able to make major names for themselves as a result of this hometown support. Local artists such as Paolo Veronese, one of the leading Renaissance painters, and Martino da Verona, one of the great fresco artists of the 14th century, thrived in this environment. The Veronese are passionate about opera and value the annual opera festival in the Arena not just as an economic bonus, but as a cultural resource. The locals snap up the best seats as soon as tickets go on sale.

Verona's civic-owned art collections are outstanding and they underscore the long history of supporting local artists. Along with the masterpieces by Bellini and Rubens in the art museum at Castelvecchio, there are galleries of modern art at the Forti Palace that continually feature contemporary artists.

Verona's churches are well cared for – which may be annoying to visitors who occasionally find the best works under canvas covers to protect them from restorations around them – and their artistic treasures appreciated by locals.

Private collectors have been generous to the city where their families made their money, and the most outstanding example is the Museo Miniscalchi-Erizzo, an elegant palazzo full of art, priceless antique furnishings and collections of everything from armour to

● *The cavernous passages of the Arena*

ivories. But culture is more than a lot of old paintings in churches and museums: it's a living and very lively part of the local lifestyle. You'll hear music of every type – opera is not the only kind heard in the Arena, which is also a venue for major popular performers on tour. Open-air concerts are often held on stages erected in Piazza Brà.

Shakespeare's work is alive and well (and not just because of Juliet), and performed at the Festival Shakespeariano in Verona's other Roman theatre. Ballet is also performed at the Teatro Romano, along with tango, flamenco and every other dance form. To join in the dancing yourself, head for the hills to one of Europe's best-loved indoor-outdoor discos, the Alter Ego Club, or head for Lake Garda where some of the towns on the Verona side seem to be solid with nightspots spilling music and people out into the streets.

At any time in Verona the music options may span from concerts by Alpine choirs to traditional folk-blues of Mississippi. The tourism board's website has a surprisingly complete listing; though it's not in the most compelling format, it is in English and has all the details, at ⓦ www.tourism.verona.it.

The tourist office in Peschiera has a week-by-week listing of what's going on around Lake Garda. Find out what's happening there and in nearby Vicenza as well by picking up a free copy of *CityLights*. Listings are in Italian, but quite easy to decipher. Few cities of its size have as many cultural offerings – especially in terms of theatre and music – as Vicenza.

The VeronaCard can be purchased at museums, churches, tobacconists and many other participating outlets. It costs €8 for a day and €12 for three days and entitles the bearer to free entry to museums, churches and other sites and free bus travel in the city.

◗ *Verona's old town sits in a loop of the Adige river*

Shopping

Smart Via Mazzini, the pedestrianised street that connects Piazza Brà and Piazza Erbe, is definitely the best address, with big-name label shops from Armani to Louis Vuitton lining the route. Prada chooses more plebeian neighbours on Porta Borsari, which is no

USEFUL SHOPPING PHRASES

What time do the shops open/close?
A che ora aprono/chiudono i negozi?
Ah keh awra ahprawnaw/kewdawnaw ee nehgotsee?

How much is this?
Quant' è?
Kwahnteh?

Can I try this on?
Posso provarlo?
Pawssaw prawvarrlaw?

My size is ...
La mia taglia è ...
Lah meeyah tahlyah eh ...

I'll take this one, thank you
Prenderò questo, grazie
Prehndehroh kwestaw, grahtsyeh

Can you show me the one in the window/this one?
Può mostrarmi quello in vetrina/questo?
Pooh oh mawstrahrmee kwehllaw een vehtreenah/kwehstaw?

This is too large/too small/too expensive
Questo è troppo grande/troppo piccolo/troppo caro
Kwestaw eh tropaw grahndeh/tropaw peekawlaw/ trawpaw kahraw

slouch itself, but has a more democratic mix of shops. For more reasonably priced clothes and other necessities, look to the two department stores UPIM and Coin. You'll find some hip streetwear along Via Roma, between Piazza Brà and Castelvecchio.

Shoes and leatherwear are the best buys, but don't expect bargains. Do expect quality – Italian gloves are among the world's finest (but be sure they are not inferior imported ones). For quality gold and silver jewellery, go to the nearby town of Vicenza, the capital of Italian silver- and goldsmithing. If you live in Europe and hope to take advantage of the generous wine allowances in the EU, head for the Valpolicella wine region (for red) or Soave (for white).

The market at Piazza Erbe is filled with food and naff souvenirs, but the weekly street markets may unearth some bargains amid the mass of low-quality imports.

Outside Verona, places such as Vicenza and the towns around the lakes have a regular schedule of weekly markets. Although filled with imports and everyday goods, these usually also have stalls where local farmers sell cheeses and food specialities and the occasional craftsman sets up shop.

WEEKLY MARKET DAYS – LAKE GARDA
Vicenza: Tuesday and Thürsday
Bardolino: Thursday
Decenzano: Tuesday
Garda: Friday
Gardone Riviera: Wednesday
Peschiera: Monday

Eating & drinking

As you travel through the countryside around Verona, you'll understand why the food there is so good. Here is some of northern Italy's best farmland, growing everything from asparagus and artichokes to corn for polenta and earthy mushrooms. From the Adriatic ports come daily selections of fresh seafood.

COUNTING EUROS

Food – and the dining experience – is central to Italian life, but it can eat a hole in a budget. Happily, you can find the same high-quality restaurants here as in Milan or Rome, but charging much lower prices. Your best bets are small family-run *trattorias* and *osterie*, where the menu may be limited but the cooking will be good.

For light meals opt for bars and cafés where you can find a sandwich or bruschetta, or shop in morning markets, such as the daily one in Piazza Erbe, buying picnic stuff to eat by the riverside. Another source of picnic foods is the PAM supermarket, just off Corso Porta Nuova, through the arch on Piazza Brà. ● Via dei Mulati 3 ● 045 803 2822 ● 08.00–20.00 Mon–Sat, 09.00–13.30, 15.00–19.00 Sun

If breakfast is not included with your room, head for a café or bar; they offer far better value than hotels. Coffee with hot milk – cappuccino or caffè latte – is drunk only at breakfast. Coffee ordered at any other time will automatically be espresso unless you specify *caffè americano*. In Italy, a bar is not just for alcoholic drinks, it's more of a café. Prices are much cheaper if you stand at the bar. If you see two prices listed for everything, the higher one is the table price.

RESTAURANT CATEGORIES

Average price of a three-course meal (without drinks)

£ up to €25   **££** between €25 and €40   **£££** above €40

DECIPHERING THE NAMES

Names for Italian eating-places can be very confusing, and there are no clear-cut definitions. A *trattoria* usually has a more limited and plainer menu than a *ristorante*. An *osteria* is a wine bar that serves snacks and sometimes a few dishes – or at least that's what they once were. Now the term's rustic charm has enticed some swankier places to adopt it. The same is true of *trattorias*, which may actually be quite pricey and smart. Look at the menu, which should be posted at the door, to see for certain. If there is no menu, expect high prices. A pizzeria usually also serves a full restaurant menu. *Cucina casalinga* indicates home-style cooking.

🔺 *Take a cooling break*

THE MENU
Menus are normally divided into courses: *antipasto* (starter), *primo* (first course, usually pasta), *secondo* (second course of fish or meat) and *dolce* (pudding). Vegetables (*contorni*) are not usually served unless you order them.

WINE WISE
Verona sits in the heart of the three wine-growing regions of Soave, Valpolicella and Bardolino, which produce both everyday table wines and several distinguished ones, such as Amarone. *Vino di tavola* served by the carafe (*vino sfuso*, literally 'loose' or from the barrel) is nearly always good, and inexpensive. You can ask to sample it first.

PRACTICAL DETAILS
Veronese dine late by northern European standards and many restaurants don't even open until 19.30 or 20.00. Lunch is served from 12.30 until 14.30 or 15.00. At weekends or in the summer or holiday seasons, choose a place for your evening meal early and book a table (or ask your hotelier to do it). Restaurants are often closed on Sundays and Mondays. The tourist office at Piazza Brà has a list (you'll have to ask for it) showing opening and closing days for individual restaurants. Finding a restaurant during August can be a challenge, as this is the traditional time for city restaurant-owners

THE BIG SMOKE
Although a large proportion of Italians smoke, Italy now has some of the strictest anti-smoking laws in Europe. Essentially you can't smoke in public buildings or enclosed spaces such as restaurants and bars. But you can still light up at outside tables.

to take a holiday, plus the middle of the opera season, so check they are open and book early if you can.

In most restaurants you can pay by credit card, although smaller *osterie* and *trattorias* may accept only cash. Tipping is appreciated, but is not a fixed amount. A 10 per cent tip is considered lavish; €3–€7 is respectable, depending on how fancy the restaurant is, and a small tip is usually added at a bar. Some restaurants, especially those in hotels, may add a service charge, listed on the bill (*servizio*), and no further tip is expected.

USEFUL DINING PHRASES

I would like a table for ... people
Vorrei un tavolo per ... persone
Vawrray oon tahvawlaw perr ... perrsawneh

Waiter! Waitress!
Cameriere!/cameriera!
Cahmehryereh!/cahmehryera!

May I have the bill, please?
Mi dà il conto, per favore
Mee dah eel cawntaw, perr fahvawreh

Could I have it well-cooked/medium/rare please?
Potrei averlo ben cotto/mediamente cotto/poco cotto, per favore?
Pawtray ahvehrlaw behn cawtaw/mehdeeyahmehnteh cawtaw/pawcaw cawtaw perr fahvawreh?

I am a vegetarian. Does this contain meat?
Sono vegetariano/vegetariana (fem.). Contiene carne?
*Sawnaw vejetahreeahnaw/vejetahreeahnah)
Contyehneh kahrneh?*

Entertainment & nightlife

There are plenty of choices for evening entertainment in Verona and around Lake Garda. Although a little knowledge of Italian helps, most younger people speak some English – some quite a lot – and if you mingle and look open to conversation, you'll soon acquire some good local contacts who can advise you on hot spots. Try

⬤ *Enjoy the casual camaraderie of the nightlife*

cruising the length of Corso Porta Borsari, from the Roman gate to Piazza Erbe or near Castelvecchio.

For a music bar in stylish surrounds, begin at M27, on Via Mazzini, or for a casual mix go to Café Monte Baldo just off the far end of Piazza Erbe – there's no music, but people there will know where to find it any night of the week. People stand in these places, which makes mixing and meeting easier. Il Campidoglio, a bit more chic, is on Piazzella Tirabosco, off Corso Porta Borsari.

Several places are near Castelvecchio: Caféxet is directly opposite it, with music and a friendly atmosphere, and not far beyond is Excalibur, with a disco and live music. For late music and food, head down the alley beside Sant'Anastasia to the piano bar at Madona Verona. Students congregate in bars and clubs near the university, across the river in Veronetta, especially at the aptly named Campus, where a pub-like atmosphere prevails and amusements include billiards, darts and board games. Verona's best-known club is out of town, in the hills overlooking the city. Alter Ego Club attracts well-known European DJs.

For more highbrow entertainment, you can catch Shakespeare or ballet at Teatro Romano (Shakespeare is performed in English with Italian subtitles); or get tickets from around €30 to hear top opera stars – under the stars. In Vicenza, Teatro Olimpico runs a constant programme of musical productions from April through to the autumn.

Something is always going on in the lake towns. In Bardolino, for example, every Friday evening in July and August concerts are held in the former Chiesa della Disciplina in Borgo Garibaldi. Stop in at any tourist office to get local schedules; the one in Peschiera will have information on the east shore towns, the one in Decenzano covers the west shore.

Sport & relaxation

With Lake Garda and the mountains so close, outdoor sports enthusiasts head north to hike, climb, sail and windsurf. Lakeside sports centres offer equipment rentals, and hiking maps are available at tourist offices. Monte Baldo, east of Lake Garda, offers trails for walkers, hikers and mountain bikers.

CYCLING

Cycling and walking paths follow the lakeshore in several places; one good one is between Bardolino and Torri del Bénaco. In both Verona and Vicenza you can rent bicycles at the left-luggage office (*deposito bagagli*) in the railway station. Elsewhere they are available from:

Lazise: Cicli Degani ❸ Piazzetta Peschiera 13 ❶ 045 647 0173

Malcesine: Bike Extreme, under the *funivia* station in Malcesine. ❶ 045 740 0105

Sirmione: Adventure Sprint ❸ Via Brescia 15 ❶ 030 919 000 ❶ 09.00–18.30

GOLF

Arzaga Golf Club has an 18-hole par-72 course, southwest of the lake, around 65 km (40 miles) from Verona. ❸ 25080 Carzago di Cavagese della Riviera ❶ 030 680 6266 ❶ www.palazzoarzaga.com

Gardagolf Country Club has three nine-hole courses par 35–6, and is also around 65 km (40 miles) from Verona. ❸ Via Angelo Omodeo 2, Soiano Del Lago ❶ 0365 674 707 ❶ www.gardagolf.bs.it ❶ Closed Mon

SAILING & WINDSURFING

Boats of all sorts are available on Lake Garda. Ask for *barca* (boat), *barca a vela* (sailing boat) or *motoscafo* (motorboat). Find a sign saying *noleggio* (for hire) and you're as good as afloat. To swim, look for small *piscina* (pool) or *spiaggia* (beach) signs along the shores, but don't expect to find sand. Lake beaches are more likely to be covered in small round stones.

Because of the more predictable winds from the mountains, Lake Garda's northern waters offer excellent sailing. Rent boats in Casteletto del Brenzone, just south of Malcesine, from Tredi Cuori Nautica. ⓐ Via Imbarcadero 17 ⓣ 045 743 0805

Especially in the spring and autumn, you will find windy days anywhere; a good sailing school for all ages (including a unique programme for children aged 3–5) is Fraglia Vela ⓐ Porto Maratona, Decenzano del Garda ⓣ 030 914 3343 ⓦ www.fragliavela.it. For windsurfing lessons: try the Windsurfing Center ⓐ Punta Caval, Torri del Banaco ⓣ 347 733 3385

SPAS

Romans built the first spa in Sirmione, taking advantage of natural thermal springs. Today Terme di Sirmione has several spa centres in Sirmione, offering different services and treatments using the sulphurous spring waters. Terme di Sirmione ⓣ 030 990 4923 (free phone in Italy) ⓣ 800 802 125 ⓦ www.termedisirmione.com. Less well known is the thermal lake in the grounds of Villa Cedri, near Lazise, with thermal fountains, a grotto and hydromassage pools. Parco Thermale del Garda ⓐ Piazza di Sopra 4, Cola' di Lazise ⓣ 045 759 0988 ⓦ www.villadeicedri.com

Accommodation

Italy's star system helps you know what to expect of a lodging's level, and is based on regular inspections. At two-star hotels, for example, most or all of the rooms will have private bathrooms; three-star establishments will have in-room telephones and television. Internet points, oddly, may be available in the most modest hotel and unavailable in a costlier one. There is usually a charge, but not always. Wi-fi is becoming more common in larger

⬤ *Stars on the sign: a good guide to hotel quality*

hotels in Verona; the San Luca, for example, offers it throughout the building, as well as a station for guest use in the lobby.

Safety is not a consideration when choosing a hotel in Verona, since there is no 'bad' section of the city. Corsa Porta Nuova, which leads from the railway station to Piazza Brà, is broad, well lit and a good area, with hotels in all price ranges.

Establish the rate when booking (always ask for special packages, especially at weekends), and request fax or e-mail confirmation. Always have confirmed bookings for August, when locals head for the lakes and foreign visitors fill the city for the Opera festival, and also for Easter week and for arrival and departure nights. Some lake hotels close between November and March.

HOTELS

Albergo Trento £ Recently completely refurbished, this small and well-positioned hotel is probably among the best bargains in town. The rooms are small but comfortable and have private bathrooms with modern facilities. @ Corso Porta Nuova 36 ☎ 045 596 444 ✆ 045 591 208

Al Quadrifoglio £ A small B&B with three rooms (one with private bathroom, two sharing) in the Borgo Trento area. Rates include breakfast – and hosts who are anxious to help you plan your excursions. @ Via XXIV Maggio 6 ☎ 338 225 3681 ✆ 045 830 0181

Catullo £ An inexpensive choice for an inner-city location, it is on the third floor and has no lift. The basic rooms are comfortable and clean but have few amenities. Private bathrooms are available. It's popular, so book early. Parking is in a car park a few streets away. @ Via Valerio Catullo 1 ☎ 045 800 2786

Franccaroli B&B £ A tiny B&B along the river, close to the mythical Juliet house and the centre of town. It has been redone recently.

🔺 *Cosy comfort in Hotel San Luca*

Book early, as it is popular. ⓐ Lungo Adige 23, Porta Vittoria ☎ 045 800 0742

Hotel Aurora ££ Situated centrally in Piazza Erbe, the Aurora has recently been renovated. The rooms are attractive, comfortable and have mod cons such at satellite TV, private phones and air conditioning. Most rooms and the terrace bar overlook the busy piazza. Car park is nearby. ⓐ Piazza Erbe ☎ 045 594 717 or 597 834 🖷 045 801 0860 ⓦ www.hotelaurora.biz

Hotel Martini, Hotel Piccolo ££ Both of these hotels are on the same street, a bit west of the central rail station. Modern, comfortable and with expected amenities. ⓐ Via Camuzzoni 2 and 3b ☎ 045 569 400 🖷 045 577 620 ⓦ www.hotelmartiniepiccolo.com

Hotel Accademia ££–£££ This recently renovated hotel is just off the main shopping street, near the main sites. Guest rooms and public areas are beautifully appointed and comfortable. Satellite TV. Parking is available. ⓐ Via Scala, 10–12 ☎ 045 596 222, 800 813 013 🖷 045 800 8440 ⓦ www.spacehotels.it, www.accademiavr.it

Hotel San Luca ££–£££ The San Luca is an elegant, refined, small (36-room) hotel with an ideal location only a few steps from the

PRICE RATINGS
Hotels in Italy are graded according to a star system (1 star for a cheap pensione to 5 stars for a luxurious resort with numerous facilities). Ratings in this book are for a single night in a double room, including breakfast.
£ up to €80; **££** €80–€140; **£££** over €140

city's centre, Piazza Brà. The hotel has covered car-park facilities with lift access to the hotel. It also has an intimate bar and a guest lounge with high-speed internet access. ⓐ Via Volto San Luca 8 ⓣ 045 591 333, 800 813 013 ⓕ 045 800 2143 ⓦ www.hotelsanluca.it

Due Torri Hotel Baglioni £££ The Due Torri is the Queen of Verona hotels. Set in a Renaissance palazzo, the rooms are all different and furnished with a Renaissance flair. Service is impeccable and the concierge service loves to make wishes come true. Tickets to the opera and a romantic dinner – poof, done! Pure class. ⓐ Piazza Sant'Anastasia 4 ⓣ 045 595 0444 ⓕ 045 800 4130 ⓦ www.baglionihotels.com

HOSTELS

Ostello Santa Chiara £ A new hostel, it is near the Teatro Romano and the Giusti Gardens. ⓐ Via Santa Chiara 10 ⓣ 045 597 807 ⓕ 045 800 9127

Ostello Villa Francescatti £ On the east side of the Adige but within walking distance of the city centre, this hostel also has camping. ⓐ Salita Fontana del Ferro 15 ⓣ 045 590 360 ⓕ 045 800 9127

CAMPING

Castel San Pietro £ An attractive area with trees overlooking the great bend of the Adige. Primarily for tents, no hook-ups to services. ⓐ Via Castel San Pietro 2 ⓣ 045 592 037 ⓦ www.campingcastelsanpietro.com

Giulietta E Romeo £ Tents and service hook-ups available. ⓐ Via Bresciana 54 ⓣ 045 851 0243

One way to be sure of a certain quality is to book rooms through affinity groups (different from hotel chains) such as Best Western, The Charming Hotels or Space Hotels. Independently owned lodgings group together in these associations to pool their marketing efforts and assure travellers of a certain level of standards. Their directories and websites have photographs and dependable descriptions.

HOTEL GROUPS
Best Western ⓦ www.bestwestern.it
Aus ⓣ 800 222 422
Ire ⓣ 800 709 101
NZ ⓣ 09 520 5418
S Africa ⓣ 011 339 4865
UK ⓣ 0800 393 130
US ⓣ 800 528 1234

The Charming Hotels
ⓦ www.thecharminghotels.com
UK ⓣ 0800 2427 6464

Space Hotels
ⓦ www.spacehotels.it
UK ⓣ 0500 30 3030
Ireland ⓣ 800 992521
US ⓣ 800 843 3311
Canada ⓣ 800 843 3311
S Africa ⓣ 861 11 9000

THE BEST OF VERONA

Whether you are on a flying visit to Verona, or taking a more leisurely break in northern Italy, the city offers some sights and experiences that should not be missed.

TOP 10 ATTRACTIONS

- **Arena** From gladiators to grand opera, this magnificent 1st-century Roman structure has seen it all (see page 78)

- **Castelvecchio** See the brilliantly designed art gallery in this grand castle setting (see page 80)

- **Giardino Giusti** A Renaissance oasis in the heart of the city (see page 60)

- **San Zeno** Verona's happy saint gazes at superbly restored frescoes, ancient graffiti and magnificent bronze panels (see page 83)

- **Santa Maria in Organo** Heavenly choirstalls and fabulous frescoes make this 15th-century church a visual feast (see page 65)

- **Piazza dei Signori** Dante's statue stands watch over this magnificent square (see page 60)

- **Castel San Pietro view** Climb to the terrace and watch the sun go down over Verona and the River Adige (see page 59)

- **Sant'Anastasia** Enjoy the Gothic splendour of this magnificent church (see page 64)

- **Arche Scaligeri** Flamboyant to the last, the ornate stone tombs of Verona's leading medieval family (see page 56)

- **Teatro Romano** Still hosting dramas after 2,000 years (see page 66)

🔽 *A view of Verona from the Roman theatre*

Here is a brief guide to seeing and experiencing the best of Verona, depending on the time you have available.

HALF-DAY: VERONA IN A HURRY

Luckily for the traveller without much time, Verona is a very compact city, with a lot of interesting sights right in the old centre. Begin at Piazza Brà, taking time to see inside the Arena before following Via Roma to Castelvecchio and the Ponte Scaligeri. Follow Corso Cavour past the fine palazzi to the Roman gate of Porta Borsari. A right turn will bring you to Via Mazzini, within sight of your starting point in Piazza Brà. Or, if you still have a little time when you reach Porta Borsari, continue through the gate to Piazza Erbe, the centre of Roman Verona. At the other end of the piazza, a right on Via Mazzini takes you along the city's most fashionable street back to Piazza Brà.

1 DAY: TIME TO SEE A LITTLE MORE

Follow the route above to Piazza Erbe, but instead of returning on Via Mazzini, go through the arch into Piazza dei Signori. Take the lift to the top of Torre Lamberti for a view over the city, or go straight on through the piazza to see the Scaligeri tombs. A left takes you to Corso Sant'Anastasia, which leads to the church of the same name; it is well worth visiting. Continue down the narrow passageway beside the church to the arcaded Via Sottariva. To the right, under the arches, is the atmospheric Osteria Sottariva, a good place to eat. A right turn at the *osteria* takes you back to Piazza Erbe.

2–3 DAYS: SHORT CITY BREAK

If you have longer to explore, venture over the Ponte Pietra to Teatro Romano and see the inlaid choirstalls at Santa Maria in Organo before continuing on to the Giardino Giusti. Or go in the other direction from Castelvecchio, along the river to the church of San Zeno. With the added time, be sure to spend some of it in a café in Piazza Brà – or in Piazza Erbe – and watch the local life go by.

LONGER: ENJOYING VERONA TO THE FULL

With more time to spend, after you have seen the highlights of Verona, head either for Lake Garda for a drive around the lower part, using the car ferry to cross from Torri de Bénaco to Maderno, or for a boat trip around the lake with an overnight stop in either Gardone Riviera, Salò or Malcesine. If it's a weekend, you might choose Desenzano to sample some of the nightlife, or spend the time in Vicenza seeing the magnificent Palladian buildings and catching a little of the nightlife there.

● *Ponte Scaligeri, built as an escape route from Castelvecchio*

Something for nothing

Shakespeare spoke of the walls that surround Verona when he had
Romeo lament of his banishment that, 'There is no world without
Verona's walls but purgatory, torture, hell itself.' Looking for the
walls and trying to piece together the original outlines of the city is
like putting together a puzzle – although this one is more like
several overlapping puzzles, all with pieces missing. Since parks now
surround the outer walls, a day spent walking the walls is also a
good excuse for a picnic.

There are not very many signs of the original Roman walls,
although some Roman gates remain. Begin in the old city centre, on
Via Capello, where a segment of pavement has been removed to
show the foundations of a huge Roman gate. One small arch of it is
built into an adjacent wall, and a sign shows how the two remnants
of the gate fitted together. A few other bits of the early Roman walls
remain: the easiest to find are Porta Borsari, at Via Diaz and Corso
Porta Borsari, and a section of the Arena.

The next significant wall-building occurred after the great
flood of 1239, when the part between Ponte Aleardi and Piazza Brà
was built. This is the most imposing stretch remaining in the city;
it once continued all the way to Castelvecchio. It is in almost
perfect condition.

The Scaligeri reign lasted until the Venetians took over in the
early 1400s. It was under the Venetians, in the 16th century, that
the architect Sanmicheli made the far-reaching plans that allowed
Verona to grow within a fortified perimeter and the outer walls
were built. You can walk these walls for some distance: the longest
segment runs from the river at Ponte San Francesco around to the
river at Ponte Catena. A park surrounds the walls here, and in this

section you will find some of the magnificent gates that Sanmichele designed as entrances to the city. These are Porta Nuova in white marble, Porta Pailo in brown tufa and Porta San Zeno in white tufa and brick. Across the river are Porta San Giorgio (or Porta Trento), made of tufa faced in white stone, and Porta Vescovo, which was enlarged in 1860, and is the site of Verona's liberation from Austria in 1866.

⬥ *Corso Porta Borsari*

When it rains

Nothing is quite so grey and glowering as a rainy day in Verona. The encouraging thing is that, except in the winter, rain is likely to leave as suddenly as it appeared.

Unlike many Italian cities, Verona's shopping streets are not protected by porticoes. But shops on Via Mazzini are close together so, unless it rains hard, you can dart between them easily.

A rain-soaked day is also a good time to savour Castelvecchio and its collections. Castelvecchio and Ponte Scaligero were built in 1354–6, but subsequent owners – Venetians, French and Austrians – made a number of changes. Napoleon added the interior courtyard. Most recently, the task of turning the already changed castle into an art museum to house the city's outstanding collections was put to the pre-eminent Venetian architect, Carlo Scarpa. His brilliant redesign not only created an excellent environment for viewing and preserving the art, but it undid some of the changes that had been made in the original castle. As the work progressed, some hidden original features were discovered, such as a door that had been sealed up centuries ago. Think of the building itself as a museum of architecture and look for his work as you tour, beginning with the modern gridwork door at the entrance.

Inside this modern gallery is a gathering of northern Italian art that spans the centuries from the Roman and Middle Ages to the 1700s (later works are in the city's other art museum, at Palazzo Forti). Works by Gothic and Renaissance painters are particularly strongly represented. The museum shows works by Stefano da Verona, Mantegna, Pisanello and Tintoretto.

The original equestrian sculpture of Cangrande that used to top his tomb has been brought here to protect it from the weather and is displayed in a setting designed by Scarpa. So concerned was he to get the setting right for this statue – one of the world's great works of 14th-century sculpture – that he made more than 600 drawings before he completed the platform and surroundings.

⬣ *Cangrande's statue now stands guard at Castelvecchio*

On arrival

TIME DIFFERENCES

Italy is on Central European Time (CET). During Daylight Savings Time (late Mar–late Oct), clocks are set ahead one hour. Italy is one hour ahead of London, six hours ahead of New York and Toronto, seven ahead of Chicago, eight ahead of San Francisco and Vancouver, eight behind Sydney, twelve behind Wellington and the same as Johannesburg.

ARRIVING

By Air

Verona's Valerio Catullo airport (☎ 048 095 666) is in Villafranca, about 16 km (10 miles) southwest of the centre. A shuttle operates every 20 minutes, 06.10–11.30, between the airport and the railway station at Porta Nuova. Tickets are approximately €6.50. ☎ 045 805 7911 ⓦ www.aptv.it. A taxi costs about €30 to the city, but can take you straight to your hotel.

Aeroporto Brescia can also be reached by shuttle bus from Verona's railway station at Porta Nuova. Frequent buses run from Brescia to Salò, on Lake Garda's western shore, and trains from Brescia access both Descenzano and Peschiera on the lake, and Verona's Porta Nuova station.

By Rail

Verona's Porta Nuova railway station is close to the city centre (within walking distance if you are not carrying luggage), and connected to Piazza Brà by bus (buy a ticket first in the bus station, opposite the railway station). To get to the centre of Verona from the station, follow the street to the right as you exit the station, through the city gate and straight ahead on Corso Porta Nuova.

By Bus

Buses arrive at Porta Nuova; the two stations face each other.

DRIVING IN VERONA

Unless you have to, avoid driving in the city. If you need a car at some point in your trip, either plan to pick it up and drop it off at the airport and use public transport into the city, or use the car rentals at the train station, convenient to major outbound routes. Cars are not allowed to drive through the central area unless you are staying in a central hotel, when you may drive in and out. Street parking is difficult, but several underground car parks are handy for the centre. One is at Piazza Cittadella, just off Corso Porta Nuovo, less than five minutes' walk from Piazza Brà. Metered parking is available along the river on Lungadige Capuleti, near Ponte Aleardi bridge. Hotels usually charge extra for parking. Routes in and out of the city are wide and well signposted.

In Italy all traffic drives on the right. If you are used to driving on the left, be very alert, particularly when you start out each day or enter a road without traffic. Ask a passenger to help by reminding you that you are driving on the right.

FINDING YOUR FEET

Verona's old centre is well kept and charming, snuggly encircled by walls and the river. Life there is lively and upbeat, especially when the weather is nice and everyone takes to the streets. Bars, cafés, restaurants, clubs, markets and shops all seem to open their doors and flow onto the well-worn paving stones of its streets, alleyways and *piazze*.

Although you should always be aware of your surroundings in any city, Verona is a relatively safe place for travellers. That said, it is

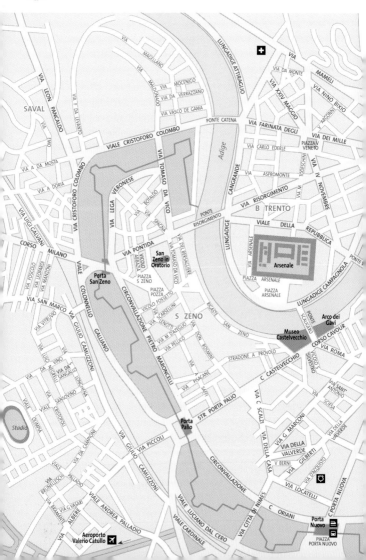

Verona

0   250 metres
0   250 yards

VIA GAZZERA
VIA SIRTORI
VIA IPPOLITO NIEVO
VIA CASTELLO S FELICE
VIA CASTELLO S FELICE
LUNGADIGE SAN GIORGIO IN BRAIDA
VIA GIORGIO IN BRAIDA
Porta San Giorgio
o Porta Trento
PONTE PIETRA
Castel
San Pietro
Teatro
Romano
Duomo di Santa
Maria Matricolare
PONTE
GARIBALDI
VIA SAN GIACOMO
VIA DUOMO
VIA PIGNA
FORTI VIA SANT'ASTASIA
VIA S CHIARA
BIONDELLA
VIA G GARIBALDI
VIA ROSA
CORSO SANT'ANASTASIA
SOTTORIVA
LUNGADIGE RE TEODORICO
VIA MARIA ROCCA MAGGIORE
VIA DI S TOMMASO
VIA CIPOLLA
PANVINIO
VIA S MAMASO
VIA FAMA
PIAZZA
DEI SIGNORI
VIA S
MARIA
IN CHIAVICA
MATTEO
Giardino
Giusti
EMILEI
VIA S
EUFEMIA
Arche Scaligere
PIAZZA
ERBE
VIA
VIA S EUFEMIA
CORSO PORTA BORSARI
VIA PORTICI
VIA V SPADE
VIA PELLA
PONTE NUOVO
PIAZZA
INDIPENDENZA
LUNGADIGE RUBELE
VIA CARDUCCI
VIA MURO PADRI
VIA S NAZARO
Porta
Vescova
VIA BARANA
Porta
Borsari
VITTORIA
VIA DIAZ
VIA OBERDAN
CORSO PORTA BORSARI
VIA CATULLO
VIA MAZZINI
VIA CAPPELLO
VIA SCALA VIA STELLA
VIA LEONI
VIA
PONTE
VIA FILIPPINI
Porta Leoni
LUNGADIGE SAMMICHELI
PONTE NAVI
VIA TREZZA
VERONETTA
VIA S NAZARO
VIA VENEZIA
Arena
VIA S
ANFITEATRO
VIA NICOLA
VIA ZAMBONI
VIA LEONCINO
STR S FERMO
VIA SATIRO
VIA S PAOLO
VIA XX SETTEMBRE
VIA NICOLA MAZZA
VIA ROTARI
PIAZZA
BRA
VIA LEONCINO
VIA DIETRO FILIPPINI
VIA MURO
LUNGADIGE PORTA VITTORIA
VIA DEL ARTIGLIERE
VIA CAMPOFIORE
TORBIDO
Stazione F S
Porta Vescovo
VIA DEGLI ALPINI
STRADONE MAFFEI
VIA MACELLO
Porta
Vittoria
University
of Verona
Palazzo Gran
Guardia
PIAZZA
CITTADELLA
VIA PALLONE
VIA MACELLO
PONTE ALEARDI
PIAZZALE
CIMITERO
VIA FRANCESCO
VIA GALILEI
VIA C MONTANARI
VIC TERESE
VIA CROCE
VIA TEZONE
LUNGADIGE CAPULETI
VIA PRETO
VIC STIMATE
VIA SAN DOMENICO
VIA
S TRINITA
VIA TRAINOTTI
VIA
ZAPPATORE
VIA BERTONI
VIA DEL PONTIERE
VIA STOPPELE
Cimitero
VIA DEL MINATORE
VIA DEL CARRISTA
VIA DEL FANTE
CIRCONVALLAZIONE RAGGIO
LUNGADIGE GALTAROSSA
PONTE SAN FRANCESCO
Adige
S PANCRAZIO
N

✝ ....Cathedral
ℹ ....Information
◉ ....Police Station
✈ ....Airport
🚉 ....Railway Stn
🚌 ....Bus Station
✚ ....Hospital

wise to avoid dimly lit streets, as well as parks or deserted areas at night. Women will rarely be hassled in Verona, and certainly less than farther south in Italy. The Veronese of all ages are polite and hospitable people who will answer your questions, give you directions and offer help.

ORIENTATION

Verona's old city is surrounded by the River Adige on three sides, and many of its key attractions are within this tightly bound area of traffic-free streets. Via Mazzini connects Piazza Brà, where the Arena is, to Piazza Erbe, and most of the streets between are pedestrianised. That area is described in this book under 'The Old Centre', with a line drawn roughly from Ponte Navi across to Ponte Vittoria. Also incuded in that section are sights on the other side of the river north of those bridges. Piazza Brà and the area around and to the south of it, as well as the long section of the city enclosed between the walls and the river west of Piazza Brà are in the second section, entitled 'The Arena and West'. Its principal sights are connected by Via Roma, which runs between Piazza Brà and Castelvecchio, and Rigaste San Zeno, which follows the river to the outstanding church of the same name, about a 20-minute walk away. San Zeno is also connected to Castelvecchio by a bus.

GETTING AROUND
Public transport

Although you won't need (or be able) to take a bus to most sights, local buses are available to San Zeno, Giardino Giusti and to the railway station at Porta Nuova. ❶ Route numbers are different on Sundays, holidays and evenings. Bus 31, 32 or 33 (Sun and hols 93) from Castelvecchio will take you to San Zeno, bus 51 or 83 (Sun and hols 92, 93, 97) runs from Piazza Brà (stopping just outside the gate at the head of Corso Porta Nuova) to the train station. City buses are easy to recognise, as all are marked AMT. Buy a ticket (approximately €1.50) from a newsstand or tobacconist before boarding and be sure to have it stamped in the machine inside the bus when you board. A daily tourist ticket costs about €4.50. ☎ 045 887 1111 ⓦ www.amt.it. Ask at the tourist office for a copy of the bus routes and schedules, and be sure to use the '*feriah*' schedules on weekdays and '*serali e festive*' on Sundays, holidays and the evenings.

Buses to Lake Garda are blue and depart from the bus station, right in front of the train station at Porta Nuova. Purchase tickets first inside the small bus station. ☎ 045 805 7911 ⓦ www.aptv.it

IF YOU GET LOST, TRY …

Excuse me, do you speak English?
Mi scusi, parla inglese?
Mee scoozee, parrla eenglehzeh?

Excuse me, is this the right way to the old town/the city centre/the tourist office/the station/the bus station?
Mi scusi, è questa la strada per città vecchia/al centro città/l'ufficio informazioni turistiche/alla stazione ferroviaria/alla stazione degli autobus?
Mee scoozee, eh kwehstah lah strahda perr lah cheetta vehkyah/ahl chentraw cheetteh/looffeechaw eenforrmahtsyawnee tooreesteekeh/ahlla stahtsyawneh ferrawvyarya/ahlla stahtsyawneh delee ahootawboos?

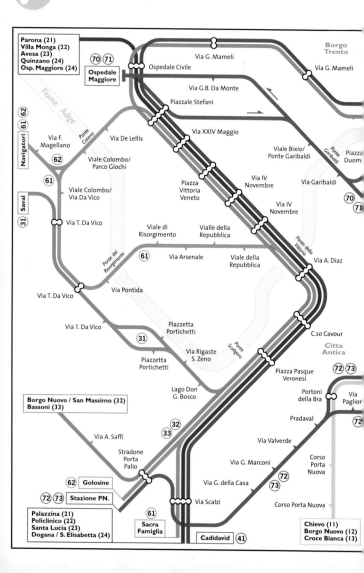

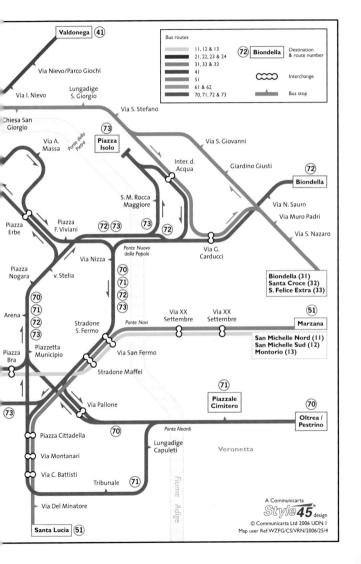

Taxis

Ranks are located at Piazza Brà, Porto Nuova rail station, Piazza Erbe and Piazza San Zeno. Radio-dispatched taxis can be called 24 hours a day. ❶ 045 532 666. Taxis are metered, and fares within the central city cost about €7–€10; there is an extra charge for luggage.

Car hire

While a car is more bother than help in the city, it is the best (and sometimes only) way to explore the surrounding areas and Lake Garda (although there are buses and even trains to the lake's principal towns). All major car-hire agencies can be found at the arrivals halls of Verona's airport. Check rates before booking your flight, because you can sometimes do best with an airline's air–car package (and often get good air rates through the car-rental office as well).

Before leaving the car park, be sure you have all documents and that you know how to operate the vehicle. Remember to drive on the right.

Car-hire offices at Verona's Valerio Catullo Airport are open 09.30–23.00.

Auto Europe ❶ UK 0800 358 1229; USA/Canada 888 223 5555

Avis ❶ 045 987 571

Hertz ❶ 045 861 9042

Car-hire offices in the railway station, Porta Nuova, are closed Saturday afternoon & Sunday.

▶ *The magnificent Arena is Italy's best preserved*

The Old Centre

This is the heart of Verona, the narrow, stone-paved streets of elegant *palazzi*, some a bit more faded and tattered than others, but all picturesque with their Venetian arched windows and often decorated with frescoes. Just wandering through these streets is a treat.

SIGHTS & ATTRACTIONS

Verona's major sights lie in a relatively small area of pedestrianised streets, so they are easy to organise into a walking route. It's a good thing, since there is no bus transport in the city centre.

Arche Scaligeri (Scaligeri Tombs)

Behind Piazza dei Signori, the ornate stone tombs of Verona's leading medieval family, the della Scala, form one of the city's major Gothic art treasures. Atop the largest and grandest of these are effigies, fully armoured and on horseback. These over-the-top Scaligeri Tombs, both dating from the 1300s, almost hide the family's church, the 12th-century Santa Maria Antica (see page 64). The tombs are always visible from outside the ornate iron fence (notice the ladder worked into ironwork pattern, the family's symbol), or you can pay admission to go inside the fence and inspect them more closely.

📍 Via Arche Scaligeri, off Piazza dei Signori ☎ 045 595 508
🕐 09.30–19.30 Tues–Sun, 13.30–19.30 Mon; admission charge (combined with Torre Lamberti)

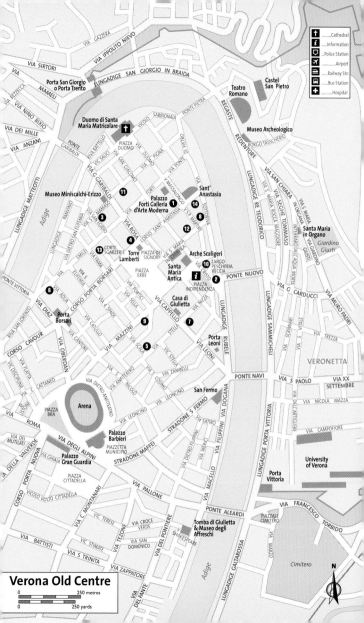

JULIET, VERONA'S URBAN MYTH

There's not a lick of truth to it, but the tragic tale of Romeo and Juliet has become the world's most enduring love story, retold in opera, ballet, film – and even a Broadway musical. But the plot did not begin with Shakespeare, or in Verona. In 1530, Luigi da Porto chose the names of two Vicenza families, the Montecchi and Capelletti, for his characters, perhaps inspired by two castles above nearby Montecchio Maggiore (see page 94). In 1562, British poet Arthur Brooke published his 3,000-line translation of the story. This drew William Shakespeare's attention, and his play, set in Verona, is considered the best version of the tale; certainly it's the best known.

Verona has a sort of love-hate relationship with these fictional residents. While shopkeepers make euros on souvenirs and hotels (even pastry shops) promote Romeo and Juliet, locals privately roll their eyes at the hordes of giggling teens and leering men who grasp the right breast of the bronze Juliet for photographs beneath the balcony (touching the statue is supposed to bring good fortune). Never mind that the balcony was put there in the 1930s by a government bent on creating its own myths, or that the house was chosen because it was once owned by a family whose name sounded something like Capulet. Try as Verona does to be honest (the city's website has a very accurate account), the myth has a life of its own.

So the Veronese shrug and play along, obligingly designating an unoccupied tomb as Juliet's and smiling indulgently as the Juliet Club (w www.julietclub.com) affixes plaques claiming buildings as locations of various scenes from the play.

Casa di Giulietta

The restored medieval building with its 1930s balcony opens into a courtyard full of chattering tourists. Its arched passageway is covered in graffiti, and the lovely bronze statue of Juliet by sculptor Nereo Costantini is kept shiny (or at least one part of it is) by hundreds of thousands of hands. Inside, the house is an interesting look at domestic architecture, with some period furnishings and cinematic memorabilia.

🅐 Via Cappello 23 🅣 045 803 4303 🅒 08.30–19.30 Tues–Sun, 13.30–19.30 Mon; admission charge (courtyard free)

Castel San Pietro

At the end of the Ponte Pietra, a stepped passageway leads up – and up – to the castle, a much-rebuilt affair that was originally built by King Theodoric, on a site that had been fortified by the Romans. The castle itself isn't open, nor is it the purpose of the climb. From the terrace before it is a smashing view of Verona, embraced snugly by the Adige. While the sunset views from any height on this side of the river are good, this is the favourite spot for the Veronese to watch their city fade into evening shadows.

🅐 Piazzale Castel San Pietro (accessed via Vicolo Botte); admission free 🅝 Bus 31 (Sun and hols 90) to stop San Giorgio

Duomo di Santa Maria Matricolare

Verona's cathedral is, like many Italian churches, a sampler of the styles current at the time of its various reconstructions – Romanesque, Gothic and Renaissance. The site is older than any of these, first a Roman temple, then a 5th-century church. What you see now was begun in 1139, and the double-storey Romanesque portal with its sombre stone saints dates from those medieval times. The cathedral's artistic highlight is in the first chapel on the left which contains Titian's 1530 *Assumption*. The choir screen, by Michele Sanmicheli (1484–1559), who designed many of Verona's palaces, is worth a look.

ⓐ Piazza Duomo ⓣ 045 595 627 ⓛ 10.00–17.30 Mon–Sat, 13.30–17.00 Sun (summer); 10.00–13.00 & 13.30–16.00 Mon–Sat, 13.30–17.00 Sun (winter); admission charge

Giardino Giusti

Counted among the finest Renaissance gardens in Italy, the 15th-century Giusti gardens are a green oasis on the east side of the river. Peaceful lower lawns with statues and parterres give way to a wilder hillside where paths climb through the trees, giving views over the neatly trimmed gardens and dark cypresses below. At the very top, a grotesque carved face forms a balcony. At one side of the lower garden is a hedge maze that few can resist pitching their wits against.

ⓐ Via Giardino Giusti 2 ⓣ 045 803 4029 ⓛ 09.00–20.00 (summer), 09.00–sunset (winter); admission charge (not included in VeronaCard) ⓝ Bus 31 or 73 (Sun and hols 90) to stop Piazza Isolo

Piazza dei Signori

Expect this truly beautiful square to be largely invisible from 2006 for a few years, as work progresses on renovating the former law courts along one side into an exposition centre. But even amid the scaffolding and canvas covers, and with a giant construction crane (Italians call this their national bird) towering over the statue of Dante, you can still see the splendid Renaissance Loggia del

● *Much of the old centre is pedestrianised*

Consiglia and some of the other elegant buildings that frame this enclosed space next to Piazza Erbe. Dante lived in Verona while he was in exile from Florence.

Piazza Erbe

More intimate and medieval in feeling than the grand Piazza Brà, this older square, surrounded by colourfully frescoed buildings, has been a marketplace for at least 2,000 years. At its centre, usually hard to see because of the market stalls that almost enclose it, the Madonna of Verona atop the fountain is a Roman statue given a halo and new holier persona in 1368. The Lion of St Mark with its book, surveying the busy market from a column at the end, is a reminder that Verona was part of the Venetian empire during the glory days of the Renaissance. Palazzo Mafei, behind the lion, is 17th century, despite the latter-day Roman gods on its façade. On weekday mornings the square is filled with food vendors, replaced by souvenir hawkers the rest of the time. At night, the surrounding cafés spill even further into the square, turning it into a giant cocktail party.

Ponte Pietra

On 25 April 1945, the retreating German army mined the ancient Ponte Pietra, along with the larger bridges over the Adige, before leaving the city. A decade later, after essential services had finally been restored, the Veronese set about reconstructing their favourite bridge from the stones they had carefully salvaged from the river. The bridge the Germans destroyed had already had a tumultuous history, with recurring floods destroying several of its arches, which were rebuilt at various times. The two arches closest to Teatro

Escape the bustle in the Giardino Giusti

Romano were Roman, the one closest to the city bank was built in 1298 and the middle two had been rebuilt in 1520. The painstaking reconstruction is faithful in every detail to the one that was destroyed. Bus 31 (Sun and hols 90) to stop San Giorgio

Sant'Anastasia

It's hard to find things in Verona that are not connected to the Scala family, since the Scaligeri had a hand in nearly everything: this church was commissioned by them around 1290 and took over a century to build. Whole sections of it were removed when Napoleonic troops pillaged the city for booty to take back to Paris, but plenty of its Gothic splendour remains, and a major restoration project has left it gleaming. Just inside the door is a pair of very unusual holy water fonts. Another highlight is the Pisanello fresco of Saint George and the Princess.

ⓐ Piazza Sant'Anastasia ⓣ 045 592 813 ⓛ 09.00–18.00 Mon–Sat, 13.00–18.00 Sun; admission charge

Santa Maria Antica

The small Romanesque church of Santa Maria Antica, consecrated in 1185, was the family church of the della Scala family, and the tomb of the patriarch Cangrande I is set into the outside wall, over the church's door. The inside is plain, except for bits of 14th-century fresco and the 13th-century frescoes inside the apse.

ⓐ Via Arche Scaligeri, behind Piazza dei Signori ⓣ 045 595 508
ⓛ 07.30–12.30 & 15.30–19.00; admission charge

Santa Maria in Organo

Although the interior of the 15th-century church is lavishly decorated in fresco work, the few visitors who seek out this church across the river head straight for the choirstalls. These are decorated with amazingly detailed inlaid wood panels created between 1477 and 1501 by the monk, Fra Giovanni da Verona. It is hard to imagine that marquetry work could be so fine as to make bird feathers look real and objects appear to be three dimensional. Scenes from old Verona alternate with simulated display cupboards filled with everyday objects; others show lifelike creatures. These panels continue in the sacristy, accessed by a door from the left of the choir. Be sure to look up at the fine frescoes that make the room appear to be galleried, with clerics and nuns watching the activity below.

ⓔ Piazza Isolo Sorge, Via San Chiara, south of the Teatro Romano **ⓘ** 045 591 440 **ⓒ** 09.00–12.00, 15.00–18.00; admission free (but you may want to leave something in the basket for the upkeep of these works of art) **ⓝ** Bus 31 or 73 (Sun and hols 90) to stop Piazza Isolo

Scavi Archeologici and Roman Gates

Whenever any building project requires excavation, new pieces of Verona's Roman past emerge from beneath its streets and buildings. The foundations of a massive Roman gate have been unearthed under Via Cappello, off Piazza Erbe, and left exposed so you can see the stonework and match it with the diagram of the whole structure on the facing wall. On the other side of the wall is one complete arch of the original gate, Porta Leoni, which had been incorporated into the side of a building.

At the other end of Piazza Erbe, Via Corso Porta Borsari leads to another original 1st-century Roman gate, Porta Borsari. Beyond, on Corso Cavour, is the Arco dei Gavi (Gavi Arch; see page 78), one of the finest examples of its period.

Teatro Romano

Two thousand years ago, Romans watched performances at this theatre built into the natural curve of the hillside; then, over the centuries, the area was built over with homes and shops until no trace of the theatre remained. In 1830, a Veronese merchant purchased the land and buildings and began the task of uncovering the amphitheatre. It is in use once again, with a summer Shakespeare festival, ballet and jazz concerts. The former monastery above houses the small Museo Archeologico (Archaeological Museum; see page 68).

ⓐ Regaste Redentore 2 ⓣ 045 800 0360 ⓛ 08.30–19.30 Tues–Sun, 13.30–19.30 Mon, until 15.00 winter and performance nights; admission charge ⓦ Bus 31 (Sun and hols 90) to stop San Giorgio

Tomba di Giulietta

In the appropriately atmospheric crypt of San Francesco al Corso, an empty stone sarcophagus has been designated as Juliet's. A series of contemporary bronze panels illustrates the story.

ⓐ Via Shakespeare (off Via del Pontiere) ⓣ 045 800 0361
ⓛ 08.30–19.30 Tues–Sun, 13.30–19.30 Mon; admission charge

Torre Lamberti (Lamberti Tower)

Rising above Piazza dei Signori and Piazza Erbe, the 84-m (275-ft) Lamberti Tower marks the location of the medieval palace used as law courts, now under major restoration. Climb the tower (if you're in good shape), or pay a euro more for the lift to look down onto the umbrellas and rooftops of Piazza Erbe and for views of the snowcapped peaks of the Dolomites.

◗ *The 14th-century Scaligeri Tombs*

🄰 Piazza dei Signori ☏ 045 803 2726 🕓 09.30–19.30 Tues–Sun,
13.30–19.30 Mon; admission charge

CULTURE

Verona's treasures, for the most part, are not collected into
museums, and even when they are, the attraction is often as much
in the setting – a fine palazzo or a crumbling convent – as in the
collections themselves.

Museo Archeologico (Archaeological Museum)

The former monastery of St Jerome, above Teatro Romano, houses the
small Archaeological Museum filled with Roman statues, reliefs,
columns, mosaics, bronzes, pottery and glass. In the tiny San Girolamo
church, part of the museum, are frescoes dating from the 15th and
16th centuries. Views down onto Verona from the museum's outdoor
terraces are best photographed in the morning, when the sun hits the
colourful old houses along the opposite river bank.

🄰 Regaste Redentore 2 ☏ 045 800 0360 🕓 08.30–19.30 Tues–Sun,
13.30–19.30 Mon, until 15.00 winter and performance nights;
admission charge 🚍 Bus 31 (Sun and hols 90) to stop Lungadige
San Giorgio

Museo Miniscalchi-Erizzo

One of the city's most overlooked museums, this delightful family
collection is housed in their late-Gothic palazzo – which is in itself
well worth seeing. The exhibits include several different collections,
each interesting on its own; taken together they form a remarkable
museum. The subjects cover archaeology, armour and weapons
of the Renaissance, ivories and porcelain, and are shown amid the

Venetian 18th-century furniture and paintings that filled the rooms. A highlight is the library and '*Wunderkammer*' of Ludovico Moscardo, a room of curiosities assembled by a 17th-century scholar and traveller. Look at the outside of the palazzo to see the original 1590 frescoes on the façade, some of which mimic architectural features – statues, niches, columns and windows.

ⓐ Via San Mamaso 2 ❶ 045 803.2484 Ⓦ www.museo-miniscalchi.it ⓛ 11.00–13.00 & 16.00–19.00 Sun–Fri (winter), 11.00–13.00 Sun–Fri, closed Sat (summer). It is advisable to check these opening times, since they are likely to change); admission charge

Palazzo Forti Galleria d'Arte Moderna (Modern Art Museum)

Regional artists of the past two centuries are featured, along with changing exhibitions of contemporary works and those in the civic collections. Good for art enthusiasts, but a likely skip for others, since there are no blockbusters here.

ⓐ Vicolo Volto Due Mori 4 (enter from Corso S. Anastasia) ❶ 045 800 1903 Ⓦ www.palazzoforti.it ⓛ 09.00–19.00 Tues–Fri, 10.30–19.00 Sat & Sun (hours may vary depending on the current exhibition); admission charge (discount with VeronaCard, see page 20)

RETAIL THERAPY

Via Mazzini is *the* street. Most of the big names – Furla, Louis Vuitton, Gucci, Armani – line either side. Prices are as high as the fashion, mitigated by twice-yearly sales from mid-July to August and again in January. Corso Porta Borsari has more of these stylish shops, but with some less pricey options, especially for shoes. On the second Saturday of each month Mercato di Sottoriva turns Via Sottoriva into an antiques market.

Clark's Shop Shoes for men and women: high fashion, high quality, high prices. ⓐ Piazza Erbe 36 ⓣ 045 800 0277 ⓦ www.clarks.it

Coin Although it's a department store, most of the departments feature women's wear and cosmetics. ⓐ Via Cappello 30 ⓣ 045 803 4321 ⓛ Mon 15.30–19.30, Tues–Sat 09.15–12.30, 15.30–19.30

De Rossi il Fornaio Look for sweet confections and all manner of packaged foods that make good gifts. ⓐ Corso Porta Borsari 3 ⓣ 045 800 2489

Dischi Volanti Whatever your taste in music, you'll be overwhelmed with the choices here. Check for shows and to find out where the music action is, too. ⓐ Via Fama 7A ⓣ 045 801 2531

Dismero If you long for the total look, you'll find yours here. ⓐ Corso Porta Borsari 53 ⓣ 045 800 7375

Enoteca Storica dal Zovo Oreste Wines in amazing array, cold-pressed olive oils from the best producers in the Lake Garda and Veneto regions and balsamic vinegar from Modena fill every corner of this shop. ⓐ Vicolo S. Marco in Foro 7 ⓣ 045 803 4369 ⓦ www.enotecadalzovo.it

Gattinoni From gritty jeans to high fashion, all the latest gear. ⓐ Via Stella 17 ⓣ 045 801 5573

ItalStyle Charactere and Cinzia Rocca for women, Pierre Cardin for men. ⓐ Via Stella 15 ⓣ 045 801 1823 ⓦ www.italstyle.it

Libreria Ghelfi & Barbato A venerable bookstore with a good selection of maps and travel books, as well as some general reading in English. ⓐ Via Mazzini 21 ⓣ 045 597 732

Love Therapy Think of this as a department store for the cool-at-heart, with Sunday shopping and everything from designer jeans to writing paper – and brands like Miss Sixty, Paramita and Kana Beach. ⓐ Via Mazzini 6 ⓣ 045 596 577 ⓛ 09.00–19.30

Mix de Lance Jeans and bags from big-name makers, such as Just Cavalli. ⓐ Via Stella 17A ⓣ 045 801 2817

Mr Gulliver From flight jackets to well-worn jeans, this retro/second-hand shop in the low-rent district across the river (take Ponte Navi) offers quirky wearables and military surplus at fair prices. And should you need to rent a 1970s costume, this is the place for you. ⓐ Via S Vitale 7e ⓣ 045 801 5642 ⓦ www.mrgulliver.net

My Collection Contemporary paintings, drawings, art prints and photography, not just for the serious collector. ⓐ Via Sottoriva 12 ⓣ 045 801 3966 ⓛ Tues–Sat 10.00–13.00 & 16.00–20.00

Prada Not all the big names are on Via Mazzini. ⓐ Corso Porta Borsàri 38–42 ⓣ 045 801 3861

UPIM Clothing for everyone, housewares and general department-store merchandise. ⓐ Via Mazzini 6 ⓣ 045 596 701 ⓛ Mon–Sat 09.00–19.30

TAKING A BREAK

Finding a café with chairs to sink into is not a problem in old Verona, where you are never far from Piazza Erbe. Many more hide in the nearby small streets and squares.

Enoteca Sant'Anastasia £ ❶ Smart environs, an outstanding selection of wines and really nice small bites to go with them. ⓐ Via Massalongo Abramo 3B ⓣ 045 801 4448

Komodo Café £ ❷ A jazzy little café with outdoor tables, good bruschette and an easy vibe. Music in the evening. ⓐ Piazzetta Pescherie ⓣ 348 256 2001

Libreria Gheduzzi £ ❸ Skim through a book while you sip your mid-morning cappuccino at this friendly café in a bookshop. ⓐ 7 Corso Sant'Anastasia ⓣ 045 800 2234

Nogara Pizza & Café £ ❹ A cool interior with curvy art deco bar and a hanging mezzanine with more tables. The pizza is good, as are the bruschette. The bar has a full cocktail list, too. ⓐ Via Scala 2 ⓣ 045 803 4717.

Le Petarine £ ❺ A little *osteria/enoteca* where you can join locals for a glass of wine – or an inexpensive lunch or bar snack. ⓐ Via San Mamaso 6A ⓣ 045 594 453 ⓛ Mon–Sat 10.00–14.30 & 17.30–21.00

San Matteo £ ❻ A former church has been converted into an informal restaurant, with self-service lunches and full table service at night. Pizza is the speciality, but other dishes are available.

ⓐ Vicolo San Matteo ⓣ 045 800 4538 ⓛ daily (a good place to go on a Sunday or Monday when many others are closed)

AFTER DARK

A university and plenty of young tourists keep Verona lively at night. After a long *aperitivo* 'hour' after work, locals head to small intimate

🔺 *Ponte Pietra, painstakingly rebuilt after the war*

osterie and *trattorias* in the streets of the old city. These are easy to spot when the weather is nice, since most extend their dining rooms into the street.

Restaurants

Don't be misled by the names – in Verona there's often little difference between a *trattoria* and a restaurant, and little *osterie* may offer some surprisingly sophisticated fare.

La Taverna £–££ ❼   A friendly little *osteria* serving duck with polenta, rabbit and other interesting dishes in an attractive setting. ⓐ Via Stella 5C ❶ 045 800 8008 ❷ Closed Mon lunch and Wed

Osteria Sottoriva £–££ ❽   Tucked picturesquely under the portico of a narrow street, with plenty of atmosphere, good food and a friendly crowd. ⓐ Via Sottoriva 10 ❶ 045 801 4323 ❷ Closed Wed

Ristorante Greppia £–££ ❾   Local specialities are updated and refined at this pleasant (and pleasantly priced) restaurant just off Via Mazzini. Cosy indoors or airy tables in the *piazzetta* on a summer evening. If the pumpkin-stuffed ravioli are on the menu, don't miss them – or try the tortellini in a mascarpone sauce. ⓐ Vicolo Samaritana 3 ❶ 045 800 4577 ❷ Closed Mon

Trattoria alla Colonna £–££ ❿   Don't be surprised to see donkey (*asino*) on the menu – it's another local delicacy – served as a sauce for the pasta or as a stew. The more conservative can find rabbit, trout and very generous portions of veal. This restaurant, near the Scaligeri Tombs, serves later than most. ⓐ Largo Pescheria Veccia 4 ❶ 045 596 718 ❷ Mon–Sat 12.00–15.30, 19.00–02.00

Trattoria alla Pigna £–££ ⓫ Put this dining room high on your list. Classy enough for a big date, its prices are low and the food excellent. Go for the *nodino di vitello con asparagi e pomodorini* – tender scallops of veal with asparagus – or for the *tagliata di manzo con rucola e grana*, slices of rare beef fillet on a bed of tangy greens with shaved cheese. Book ahead at weekends, since locals fill it fast. ⓐ Via Pigna 4 ⓘ 045 800 0492 ⓒ Closed Sun & Mon.

Trattoria al Solito Posto £–££ ⓬ Home-cooked favourites and more innovative dishes fill the ever-changing menu. All the desserts are made right there, including the honey cake. Look for daily specials, midday at about €16, evenings at about €19 for a full meal. ⓐ Via Santa Maria in Chiavica 5 ⓘ 045 801 4220 ⓒ Closed Tues in winter

Osteria Sgarzerie ££ ⓭ Traditional dishes, including the hard-to-find *ossobuco alla milanese* – savoury braised veal shanks – and carpaccio of smoked horsemeat (a Veronese speciality). Begin with a delectable grilled radicchio with monte cheese or the *ravioli de zucco* with butter and sage. ⓐ Corte Sgarzerie ⓘ 045 800 0312

Due Torre £££ ⓮ For a big night out, pull out all the stops and go for broke at this elegant dining room in a Renaissance palace. Service is as good as the menu, which changes often to highlight local vegetables, meats and seafood. The lamb chops are always excellent, as is the daily risotto. ⓐ Piazza Sant' Anastasia 4 ⓘ 045 595 ⓘ booking essential

Cinemas & theatre

Corallo Digital A good choice for music-heavy cinema when the sound is particularly important, with shows as late as midnight. ⓐ Via IV Spade 19 ⓘ 045 595 990

Teatro Romano From Shakespeare to tango, the outdoor Roman theatre is used for summer productions. ⓐ Regaste Redentore 2 ⓣ 045 806 6485

Bars, clubs & discos

Two popular meeting places in this part of the city are at either end of Corso Porta Borsari: Piazza Erbe, where cafés and bars spill out onto the street in the evening, and near the Roman gate at the opposite end of the street. Cruise the street to find the night's most lively spots, and look down the tiny side streets, where other popular bars hide.

Alter Ego Club Even people who have never been to Verona have heard of this club. It's the city's most hip and edgy, although the view from the terrace in the summer is more like schmaltzy romantic, overlooking the city lights from the northern hills. Hear top Euro DJs here, though it will mean a taxi ride if you haven't got a car. ⓐ Via Torricelle 9 ⓣ 045 915 130 ⓛ 23.30–04.00 Fri & Sat

Caffè delle Erbe While you would expect a café with tables reaching into Piazza Erbe to be the haunt of tourists, it's actually an after-hours favourite of the 30-something set, who go for the good cocktails, good company and, in the summer, for the live jazz. It's quieter during the daytime. ⓐ Piazza delle Erbe 32 ⓣ 045 591 403 ⓛ 07.30–02.00 Tues–Sun

Caffè Monte Baldo This very popular and casual wine bar has a friendly crowd that spans all ages and a good list of wines in all price ranges. Little tables are in the front and bigger booths in the back room, but most stand at the bar or in the street. Nibble on *tartine*, little bread slices with various toppings. ⓐ Via Rosa 12 (near Piazza Erbe) ❶ 045 803 0579 ⓛ Closed Wed

Enoteca Segreta The classy little late-night wine bar just off Via Mazzini is hard to spot in the summer, when it is almost hidden by the tables of the neighbouring restaurant, Greppia. Nice, small plates of food accompany the wine. ⓐ Vicolo Samaritana 10 ❶ 045 801 5824 ⓛ 19.00–02.00

Il Campidoglio Not very many tourists find this chic, friendly local bar, although it's only a few steps off Corso Porta Borsari. ⓐ Piazzella Tirabosco 4 ❶ 045 594 448

M27 Stylish and upmarket (this is, after all, Verona's most fashionable street), this very popular wine and music bar is also a disco. It serves the best (and maybe only) club sandwiches in town. ⓐ Via Mazzini 27 ❶ 045 800 1339 ⓛ until 02.00 Tues–Sun

Madona Verona A stylish little piano bar that serves light food into the wee hours, it's a perfect spot for a romantic after-dinner stop. ⓐ Via don Bassi 4, beside the Due Torre Hotel and Sant' Anastasia ❶ 045 595 040 ⓛ 12.00–15.00 & 18.00–04.00

Osteria del Bugiardo A few tables and simple menu of local dishes, but most go for the wine bar. ⓐ Corso Porta Borsari 17A ❶ 045 591 869 ⓛ Closed Mon

The Arena & West

Elegant, spacious Piazza Brà marks the boundary between the close-set old streets and lanes of the old city and the broader avenues of the later city to its south. Free from the constriction of the river's tight bend, this area has a more open feel to it.

SIGHTS & ATTRACTIONS

Not so closely packed as those of the old centre, attractions here are at least connected by bus lines, easy to use in Verona as long as you remember to buy your ticket before boarding (at newsstands or bars) and to validate it in the machine as soon as you board.

Arco dei Gavi

Close to Castelvecchio on Corso Cavour is the Arco dei Gavi (Gavi Arch), a 1st-century Roman gateway complete with its pavement, showing the grooves made by chariot wheels passing through it. You may wonder why there was so much traffic through a gate that led right into the river; the gate was not originally beside the river, but was disassembled and was reconstructed here in the 1930s.

Arena

Standing at the top tier of the immense Arena (it held over 22,000 people when it was built in the 1st century AD) and looking down – way down – into the ring where gladiators once fought for their lives, it's easy to imagine the glory that was Rome. Whether you side with the lions or the Christians, you cannot help but think of the enormity of the spectacle and of the events that took place here as

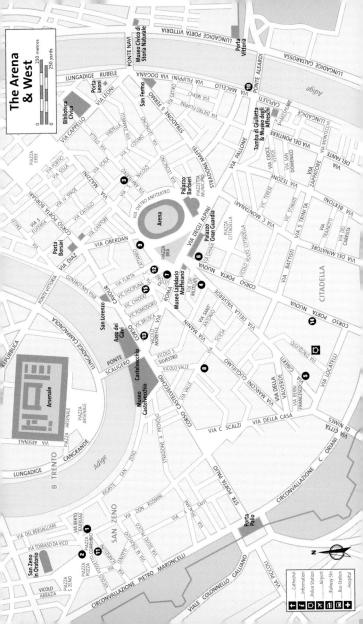

you stand in Italy's best-preserved Roman arena. It has been part of the city's history ever since, providing shelter from invading barbarians and, since 1913, providing a venue for one of Europe's most renowned summer opera festivals, the Stagione Lyrico di Verona, and major music events of all genres.

ⓐ Piazza Brà ⓣ 045 800 3204 ⓦ www.arena.it ⓛ 08.30–19.15 Tues–Sun, 13.30–19.15 Mon, opera days 08.15–15.30; admission charge ⓝ Bus 51 or 83 (Sun and hols 92, 93, 97) from Stazione Porta Nuova

Castelvecchio and Ponte Scaligero

Cangrande II (this translates as 'big dog', an accurate title, since he was top dog of the Scaligeri clan) built his impressive brick castle on the River Adige between 1355 and 1375 to secure his iron grip on the city after a revolt led by his half-brother. Connecting the castle to the other side of the river is Ponte Scaligero, castellated to make it easier to defend. It stood as one of the world's finest examples of 13th-century engineering, until the night of 25 April 1945, when the retreating German army mined it. Like Ponte Pietra, it was painstakingly rebuilt after the war from the original materials salvaged from the river. To house one of Italy's premier art museums (see page 84), the castle interior was brilliantly redesigned as an art gallery by Venetian architect Carlo Scarpi.

ⓐ Corso Castelvecchio (end of Corso Cavour) ⓣ 045 594 734

Corso Cavour Palazzi

Corso Cavour parallels the river between Castelvecchio and Ponte Vittoria, its relatively short length lined by distinguished palaces of Veronese nobility. The top of Palazzo Canossa, at No 44, is lined with statuary and the current Banca d'Italia building has caryatids on the façade. Palazzo Carlotti, at the corner of

Via Diaz, near the Porta Borsari gate, is one of Verona's few late baroque palaces.

Piazza Brà

If Piazza Brà were any smaller, the massive Arena would overwhelm it. But the leafy park in the middle – surrounded by the Palazzo Barbieri (now the municipal building), the older Palazzo Gran Guardia, and a graceful curving line of 19th-century buildings whose stately porticoes and awnings shelter a long arc of cafés – combine to create a balanced and well-used public drawing room for the Veronese. The arched gateway, Portone della Brà (look for the Shakespeare quote, 'there is no world without Verona's walls', carved into its right side) and its octagonal tower are the finishing flourish. This is *the* place to promenade in the evening or at a weekend, and to watch the Veronese as they stroll through on their way to or from Via Mazzini or as they relax in a café.

San Fermo

Several surprising treasures hide in this little-visited church near the river, but its newest masterpiece is visible any time. A series of exceptional contemporary bronze panels decorates the front doors. From inside on the right, a doorway leads down to an earlier church, which became the crypt for the present church that the Benedictines began building over it in 1070. Frescoes from the 7th and 8th centuries decorate its walls and columns. The upper church is also decorated in frescoes, but its most surprising artistic feature is hidden in the fine barrel-vaulted wooden ceiling (see the model in the nave to see the clever medieval engineering that holds this in place). Way up there is a 'colonnade' with painted panels, each with a portrait – some 416 of them. The red marble pulpit dates from 1396.

ⓐ Via Dogana 2 (at Stradone San Fermo) ☎ 045 800 7287
🕒 10.00–18.00 Mon–Sat, 13.00–18.00 Sun (summer); 10.00–13.00,
13.30–16.00 Mon–Sat, 13.30–17.00 Sun (winter)

San Lorenzo

Begun in 1110, this Romanesque church is remarkable for its rare
women's galleries (few of these survive today, although they were
common in churches of the Middle Ages) and for its red marble
door, which dates from the Renaissance.

ⓐ Corso Cavour 28 ☎ 045 800 1879 🕒 10.00–18.00 Tues–Sat,
13.00–18.00 Sun (summer); 10.00–13.00 & 13.30–16.00 Tues–Sat,
13.30–17.00 Sun (winter); admission charge

San Zeno in Oratorio

Most saints depicted in religious art look profoundly bored,
uncomfortable, in a trance or downright dour. Not Verona's San
Zeno, the African bishop who converted the city to Christianity in
the 4th century. The polychrome statue of San Zeno in his church
shows him smiling, perhaps at the fine job of restoration and
preservation that's going on around him. The frescoes on the
walls are freshly cleaned, their colours strong and clear, as is the
graffiti inscribed in some of them, autographs of pilgrims and
visitors from as far back as the 1600s (look on the wall to the
right of the altar, in the frescoes by Veronese). In the lower church,
the saint's remains lie in a glass casket. Built in the early 1100s,
San Zeno ranks high as one of the finest examples of Italian
Romanesque building to survive. Some of the 48 magnificent
bronze panels on the front doors illustrating biblical scenes and
the life of San Zeno are older than the present church. Legend
holds that the Frankish King Pepin is buried beneath the bell tower.

He is known to have been there for the consecration of the original church in 807.

ⓐ Piazza San Zeno, west of Piazza Brà, near Porta San Zeno
ⓘ 045 800 6120 ⓒ 08.30–18.00 Mon–Sat, 13.00–18.00 Sun (summer); 10.00–13.00 & 13.30–16.00 Mon–Sat, 13.30–17.00 Sun (winter) ⓦ Bus 31, 32 or 33 (Sun and hols 93) to stop Via T. Da Vico

Verona's walls

While Verona's central location on the crossroads of trade routes made it an important city, the same routes that made trade easy also put Verona in the path of invaders. The sharp curve in the river

ⵔ *San Zeno is a superb example of Romanesque architecture*

provided some natural defence, but not quite enough, so the Veronese reinforced this natural protection with successive lines of sturdy walls. Still unusually complete for a city of its size, these date from the 12th and 13th centuries. Portone della Brà, at the southern end of Piazza Brà, is the most striking reminder of the early walls. Five 16th-century gates, part of the outer defence system that survives intact around the southern and western sides of the city, make impressive entrances.

CULTURE

As if the art in Verona's churches and public buildings, and its annual opera festival weren't enough culture for one small city, Verona also has one of Italy's most outstanding art museums, housed in its Scaligeri castle (see below). An active art school, the Accademia de Belle Arti Signaroli (Ⓦ www.accademiacignaroli.it), has schools of painting, sculpture and the rare art of fresco painting. You can visit these studios in the Accademia's palazzo on Via Montanari to watch tomorrow's maestri at work.

Museo Castelvecchio
The Scaligeri castle, built in the 1300s, was adapted by architect Carlo Scarpi to house the city's remarkable collections of art, dating from the time of the Lombards, through the Middle Ages and into the 19th century (later works are exhibited in the Palazzo Forti branch of the civic museum – see page 69). The free gallery-by-gallery guide helps you find those that interest you most, but if you have time to walk through the whole museum, it is a good introduction to the progression of art styles and techniques over almost two millennia. Artists represented here include Bellini,

Pisano, Rubens, Tintoretto, Tiepolo and Guardi; much of it has been collected from palaces, churches and monasteries in Verona and the province. It is considered among Italy's best museums.

🅐 Corso Cavour ❶ 045 806.2611 🕐 08.30–19.30 Tues–Sun, 13.30–19.30 Mon; admission charge

Museo Civico di Storia Naturale

The Lessina Mountains north and east of Verona is one of the world's richest areas in plant and animal fossils, and this museum's pride is its outstanding collection of these.

🅐 Lungadige Porta Vittoria 9 ❶ 045 807 9400 🕐 09.00–19.00 Sat–Thur, closed Sun am (winter), 13.00–17.30 Sat–Thur, closed Sun am (summer); admission charge 🚌 Bus 31 or 73 (Sun and hols 90) to Piazza Isolo

Museo degli Affreschi

Although its claim to 'fame' is as the site of Tomba di Giulietta (Juliet's tomb – a purely fabricated attraction), the fresco museum through which you must walk before reaching the tomb is well worth the trip to this corner of town. In the 16th century, Verona had literally hundreds of houses whose exteriors were decorated with frescoes. Many of these were quite detailed and elaborate, others had more simple friezes, or bands of design along their tops. You can still see some of these in the old city, but only in this museum do you sense what the city must have looked like. A model of a silk trader's house shows the placement of the paintings that were saved from it, and another room is lined entirely with the frescoes from a 16th-century palace.

🅐 Via Shakespeare (off Via del Pontiere) ❶ 045 800 0361 🕐 08.30–19.30 Tues–Sun, 13.30–19.30 Mon; admission charge

Museo Lapidario Maffeiano

Stones, pure and simple, retrieved from ruins and excavations of Roman Verona form the basis of this collection. They give just a hint of what the city must have looked like 2,000 years ago. Other collections include stonework of the ancient Greeks, Etruscans and others. It's not for everyone.

ⓐ Piazza Brà 28 ⓘ 045 590 087 ⓛ 09.00–14.00 Tues–Sun, 13.30–19.30 Mon; admission charge

RETAIL THERAPY

This is not Verona's prime shopping area – in fact, there are few shops here except for along the streets just behind the Arena and the everyday shops in the outlying residential neighbourhoods. The exception is Via Roma, which runs from Piazza Brà to Castelvecchio, and some smaller streets in this area. Most of the shops here close all day Sunday and on Monday morning.

Anna Maria Chef If you love your kitchen, treat it to something shiny and new from this emporium of cookery supplies. ⓐ Dietro Listone 10A, off Piazza Brà

Città del Sole Toys for big kids, as well as little ones, with gadgets, telescopes, puzzles and hi-tech stuff in addition to the expected wooden toys and kiddie stuff. ⓐ Via Cattaneo 8b ⓘ 045 591 761

Linus The no-leather store: quality high-fashion shoes, bags and accessories in alternative materials, at good prices, just off Piazza Brà. ⓐ Via Teatro Filarmonico 3 ⓘ 045 801 0922

New Energy Energie is just one of the popular brands of this smart new clothes shop. ❷ Via Roma 18

Novella Hit the street looking like you live here, with trendy designer rags, accessories and jewellery from Italian makers.
❷ Via Cattaneo 18 ❶ 045 595 670

Territorio Dada Via Roma is full of small hip shops, and this one has casual styles and the all-time comfy stuff like World Tribe.
❷ Via Roma 26a

Vibra Hip-hop dress and music to match, for both sexes. Choose a CD, then the clothes and shoes to go with it. ❷ Via Cattaneo 15a
❶ 045 800 7006

TAKING A BREAK

Bar Café Mastino £ ❶ Sandwiches and bruschette make a good lunch or snack after visiting nearby San Zeno.
❷ Via Berto Barbiani 17A

Gelateria San Zeno £ ❷ Good for a quick pick-me-up after the walk to San Zeno, with plenty of frosty flavours to choose from.
❷ Piazza Corrubio 20

Luna Café £ ❸ Lunch specials include a first course of gnocchi, mushroom lasagna or other pasta, a drink and coffee for approximately €9.50.
❷ Via Anfiteatro 6C, behind the Arena

Pasticceria Barini £ ❹ Luscious pastries and confections, including delectable little biscuits called Baci di Giulietta (Juliet's kisses), in a classy setting just through Portone della Brà. ⓐ Corso Porta Nuova 8 ❶ 045 803 0449 ⓦ www.pasticceriabarini.it

Retrogusto £ ❺ Cheese and food shop with a small café where you can sample wondrous cheeses from all over Italy, along with other delectable treats, for lunch. ⓐ Via Berni Francesco 1 (at the corner of Via Giberti) ❶ 045 800 2167

Torre 5 £ ❻ Smart pizzeria with whopping salads and generously topped pizzas, also just outside the Portone della Brà gate. ⓐ Corso Porta Nuova 9 (enter from Via Ghiaia) ❶ 045 597 832

AFTER DARK

Piazza Brà and the area between it and Castelvecchio are the hot districts to visit at night, and across the river, near the university, are a lot of student hangouts. On a summer evening, be sure to book ahead or stake out your table early in this area, especially if you want to sit outdoors.

Restaurants
Brek £ ❼ Fast food with a twist: impeccably fresh ingredients are cooked to order after you select them yourself. You can also concoct your own salad. It's a chain restaurant, but of high quality and low price. ⓐ Piazza Brà 20 ❶ 045 800 4561

Al Ristori £–££ ❽ Tucked away in a hard-to-find *piazzetta* off Via Manin, this little *trattoria* serves its own smoked salmon and swordfish, homely dishes like *pasta e faggioli* and tender veal scallops in saffron cream. Fixed-price complete lunches are a bargain here. ❷ Vicolo Valle 1 ❶ 045 801 4685 ⏱ Closed Mon & Sun evening

Costa in Brà £–££ ❾ Despite its prime location in Verona's best people-watching spot, prices at this Piazza Brà favourite are quite reasonable. Try ravioli with smoked ricotta and poppy seeds for a starter. The long pizza menu offers some interesting toppings. ❷ Piazza Brà 2 ❶ 045 507 468

No 5 £–££ ❿ In a sleek modernist setting of red, white and chrome, this riverside restaurant serves excellent pizza, crispy seafood *fritto misto* (mixed fry) and a creative menu of other dishes at lunch and in the evening. ❷ Via Macello 5 ⏱ Closed Mon

Rosa Blu £–££ ⓫ Pizza from the wood-fired oven is a speciality, but the restaurant is far more than that, with a full kitchen that

▲ *The walls of Castelvecchio*

excels with fish dishes. Close to San Zeno. ⓐ Piazza Corrubio 29
ⓣ 045 803 6731

Ciopeta ££ ⑫ This reliable, mid-range restaurant, hidden just
off Piazza Brà, tends to be more crowded at lunch than at dinner.
ⓐ Vicolo Teatre Filarmonico 2 ⓣ 045 800 6843

Osteria Casa Vino ££ ⑬ Begin with their cheese pie with braised
leeks or assorted vegetables – it's a speciality of this historic *osteria*.
So is the traditional rabbit cacciatore. The mains are more meat-
than seafood-based. ⓐ Vicolo Morette 8 ⓣ 045 800 4337

Trattoria Malavoglia ££ ⑭ If you long for the simple joys of pasta
in red sauce in this land of polenta and butter, look no further. You'll
find hearty Sicilian fare here, along with mains of well-prepared
seafood. ⓐ Corsa Porta Nuova 46 A ⓣ 045 800 0534

Enoteca Cangrande ££–£££ ⑮ The constantly changing short menu
is a nice mix of traditional and modern (perhaps cannelloni
wrapped like crepes around a filling of porcini and truffles with an
excellent fontina cheese) and the dishes are nicely prepared and
artistically served. Be careful of the 'extras', which can add up fast at
inflated prices here, such as mineral water and coffee at double the
usual price – order your after-dinner coffee elsewhere. ⓐ Via Listone
19d ⓣ 045 595 022

Cinemas & theatres
Arena di Verona The big venue for top music performances is the
Roman Arena, which is also the site of the annual summer opera
festival from late June to August. ⓐ Piazza Brà 28 ⓣ 045 805 1811 for

schedules. Box office: Via Dietro Anfiteatro 6b ☎ 045 800 5151 🔵 www.arena.it

Astra Cinema on the street between Piazza Brà and Ponte Vittorio, playing new releases, some in original language, most dubbed into Italian. ☎ Via Oberdan 13 ☎ 045 596 327

Filarmonico The city's oldest cinema house and also its most popular, busy at weekends from early afternoon until the last show at midnight. ☎ Via Roma 2 ☎ 045 596 826

Fiume Classics and new international cinema releases in a spacious theatre that's just been updated. Films are shown outdoors in the summer. ☎ Via Porta San Zeno ☎ 045 800 2050 🚌 Bus 31, 32 or 33 (eve, Sun and hols 93) from Castelvecchio

Rivoli The latest films are screened here first. ☎ Piazza Brá ☎ 045 908 55

Bars, clubs & discos

Venues are scattered, several of them near San Zeno, with student hangouts in Veronetta, off Via XX Settembre. You can take a bus to these, but you'll have to walk home or take a cab.

Al Mascaron Laid-back cocktail and wine bar with occasional live music. ☎ Piazza San Zeno 16 ☎ 045 597 081 🕐 until 02.00 🚌 Bus 31, 32 or 33 (eve, Sun and hols 93) from Castelvecchio.

Caféxet There's always a crowd in this small wine and music bar with a mission – to be a home-from-home for anyone who seeks good company. Along with a proper cup of tea and an English breakfast, they serve a mean cup of coffee, good snacks and more substantial food. But most go for a glass of wine, good music and good vibes. ⓐ Corso Castelvecchio 5 ☎ 045 595 121

Campus As the name suggests, this place is popular with students from the nearby university who enjoy the long beer list, low prices and plentiful cheap snacks. Billiards and other games are on offer. ⓐ Via XX Settembre 18 ☎ 045 800 1549 🕐 until 04.00 Fri & Sat until 02.00 Mon–Thur

Casa del Krapfen Only in Italy... This bakery opens from 23.00–01.00 on weeknights and 03.00–05.00 on Saturday morning for those who want a bite of something sweet and an espresso before heading home after a night's drinking. It's open normal daytime hours, too. Look for it along the river over Ponte Navi. ⓐ Lungadige Porta Vittoria 15 B ☎ 045 800 4877

Excalibur Disco, bar, live-music venue, restaurant – you name it, it's here. The crowd of 20-somethings keeps it hopping after midnight, though it's always pretty busy, even before then. There's a small entrance fee. ⓐ Stradone Provolo 24 ☎ 045 597 858 🕐 21.00–03.30 Thur–Sat

Pasion Espanola Smart, friendly little tapas bar far from the tourist route, but not far from Piazza Brà (follow Via Manin from Via Roma). ⓐ Via Marconi Guglielmo 4 ☎ 045 596 038 🕐 20.00–03.00 Sun–Thur, 20.00–04.00 Fri–Sat

---

▶ *Lake Garda from Malcesine's castle*

OUT OF TOWN
trips

Around Verona

Verona sits between the gentle landscapes of the wide Po River valley and the Lessini Mountains, the steeply rising foothills of the Dolomites. Small villages with hilltop castles, dramatic natural wonders and two of Italy's best-known wine regions – Soave and Valpolicella – are within easy reach. So easy, in fact, that visitors with cars often choose to stay in one of these outlying towns and visit Verona's sights on day trips.

SIGHTS & ATTRACTIONS

Montecchio Maggiore

The trail of Romeo and Juliet begins at the twin Scaligeri castles that, according to local lore, inspired Luigi da Porto to write the original story: he could see them from his villa. Turn just before the church in the centre of town to follow signs upwards to the two castles. One of the great Palladian-style villas (see Vicenza, page 106) is nearby, set in a park-like garden. Villa Cordellina-Lombard was built in the early 1700s, with large Tiepolo frescoes in the central reception hall.

❸ Via Lovara 36 ❶ 0444 696 075 ❹ 09.00–13.00 Tues–Fri, 09.00–12.00 & 15.00–18.00 Sat & Sun (summer).

Soave

Few towns remain as snugly enclosed by their original walls as Soave, whose castle climbs in stages up the hillside behind it. Inside a medieval courtyard on the main street is the wine cellar and *enoteca* of the Coffele family, where you can sample and buy fine white, sweet and sparkling Soave.

ⓐ Via Roma 5 **ⓣ** 0457 680 007 **ⓦ** www.coffele.it. Just up the hill is the Palace of Justice, built in 1375, and a 1411 Venetian Gothic house. The castle, La Rocca, is open to the public (you can picnic inside the grounds and climb the crenellated walls) **ⓐ** Via Castelli **ⓣ** 045 786 0036 **ⓛ** Tues–Sun

Solferino

In 1859, Italians were fighting to be free of Austrian rule, and one of the most costly battles of that war was fought at Solferino. The loss of life on both sides was staggering – more than 40,000 dead or injured. A Swiss, Henry Dunant, was so moved by the sight that he began a crusade that led to the founding of the International Red Cross. Now the serene and sobering Capella Ossaria commemorates those of both armies who lost their lives here, its walls lined with skulls and bones of the dead.

Capella ⓣ 0376 854 019 **ⓛ** 08.30–12.30, 14.00–18.30 Tues–Sun, closed Mon. Below is the small but interesting Museo Storico (see Culture, page 99).

Valeggio & Borghetto

When the local silk industry declined, local women saved Valeggio by opening small restaurants and making pasta: they put tortellini on the map. Less than 32 km (20 miles) from Verona, Valeggio soon became a popular place for Veronese to go for dinner. They later restored the abandoned mill village of Borghetto, set picturesquely at a bend in the river: its restaurants, cafés and boutiques fill with locals at weekends.

Crossing the Mincio River above Borghetto is a long fortified bridge, Ponte Visconteo, built in 1393, and above it the restored Castello Scaligeri, with views all the way to the Dolomite

Mountains. You can enter the castle free any time. Castle tower
🕒 09.00–12.00, 14.30–19.00 Sun & hols. The beautifully landscaped
flower gardens and woodlands of Parco Giardino Sigurta lie below
the castle. Walking is the best way to see it, but a tourist train also
does tours through the park. 📞 0456 371 033 🌐 www.sigurta.it
🕒 09.00–19.00 (last entry 18.00) (summer); admission charge

🔺 *The Capella Ossaria at Solferino*

Valpolicella wine region

Little wineries dot the rugged landscape, and villas and their gardens add to the attraction of some of these. Some wineries need a call ahead so they can prepare food to accompany a tasting and, in the case of the Bertrani Winery in Novare, arrange for you to tour the interior of the villa, whose central hall is decorated in beautiful frescoes in almost perfect original condition. Expect to pay for tastings at larger estates, especially those that include food and tours. **Villa Mosconi-Bertani, Novare (Negrar)** ① 045 601 1211 ② 09.00–12.00 & 14.00–18.00 Mon–Fri, 09.00–12.00 Sat

Also in Negrar, the 18th-century **Villa Rizzardi** is surrounded by the beautiful Italianate and English Gardens of Pojega, created in the late 1700s, with a garden amphitheatre, fountains and waterfalls. ① 045 721 0028 ⓦ www.guerrieri-rizzardi.it ② 15.00–19.00 Apr–Oct; admission charge

Nearby **Casa Vinicola Sartori** offers wine tastings and smaller gardens to tour. ⓐ Via Casette 2, Negrar ① 0456 028 001. In Pedemonte you can visit the **Tommasi Winery**, an historic estate. ⓐ Via Ronchetto 2, Pedemonte ① 0457 701 266. Look for signs to other wineries that hold tastings or show the winemaking process, all mechanised now.

One of the prettiest towns in the region is the hilltop **San Giorgio**, north of Sant' Ambrogio, with a Longobard Romanesque church, Pieve San Giorgio. The tiny cloister beside the church is exquisite, and a little museum has Roman and earlier artifacts.

Molina Parco delle Cascate (Molina Falls Park), north of Fumane, is a large area with nature trails along gorges to several splendid waterfalls, and to caves. ⓐ Via Bacilieri ① 0457 702 185 ⓦ www.cascatemolina.it ② 09.00–19.30 (summer), 10.00–18.00 Sun (winter); admission charge

Less well known, but well worth searching out is the large (in fact, it's Europe's largest) natural bridge of Ponte di Veja, which once formed the opening to a cave where artifacts from prehistoric cave dwellers living 100,000 years ago were discovered. The arch is 29 m (90 ft) high, and you can walk across the top. You can see an amazing collection of the prehistoric finds and fossils at Museo Preistorico e Paleontologico in nearby Sant'Anna d'Alfaedo (see Culture, below).

It is possible to take tours of the Valpolicella wineries from Verona. A nine-hour wine tour typically explores the food, wines and scenery of the region, including at least one full tasting, usually with an English-speaking sommelier. Tours are offered by Avventure Bellissime ❶ 041 520 8616 ❿ www.tours-italy.com and by Italy and Wine ❶ 347 923 5359 ❿ www.italyandwine.net

CULTURE

Museo Preistorico e Paleontologico

Prehistoric artefacts found locally and fossils – including a 7-m (23-ft) shark that's 70 million years old – are displayed and interpreted in this small museum.

ⓐ Pzza dalle Bona, Sant'Anna d'Alfaedo ❶ 045 532 656
❿ www.lessiniamusei.it ❶ 09.30–12.30 & 15.30–18.30 Tues–Sun (summer), 10.00–12.00 & 15.00–17.00 Wed, Sat & Sun (winter); admission charge

Museo Storico

The simple museum near the Ossario exhibits memorabilia, uniforms and arms, including cannons, from the battle of Solferina, along with information that puts it into its historical context.

📍 Piazza Ossario, Solferino ☎ 0376 854 019 🕐 08.30–12.30 &
14.00–18.30 Tues–Sun; admission charge

RETAIL THERAPY

Soave's main street has several small shops worth browsing, and
the Borgetto area of Valeggio has some craft studios and boutiques.
Antiques fairs are popular in the region, with regular monthly dates,
usually from March to November. Look for signs for Mercantino
dell'Antiquariato in the following towns:

Soave: Third Sunday of each month
Solferino: Second Sunday of each month
Valeggio: Fourth Sunday of each month

TAKING A BREAK

Ai Parcheggi £ At the entrance to the waterfall park at Molina, this
café/bar is a good place to rest up from the trails. 📍 Parco della
Cascate, Valpolicella ☎ 0457 720 078

Bottega del Caffè £ A serious coffee bar, with a long list that
includes the sinfully delicious Caffè Nocciolato. The selection
of fresh fruit juices is just as impressive: try orange-kiwi-apple.
📍 Via Stazione 49, Alte Monteccio Maggiore

Casa Blanca Café £ There are cosy booths in the back room, but
locals drink their Soave standing at the bar to be closer to the buffet
of tasty snacks – focaccia, anchovies, marinated olives, meatballs

▶ *The mill village of Borghetto, Valeggio*

and peperoncini – offered late in the afternoon. ⓐ Via Roma 27, Soave ⓣ 045 768 0673

Enoteca Il Drago £ Simple pasta dishes or a plate of salami, cured meats and cheese goes well with a little local wine, sold by the glass so you can sample a variety. ⓐ Via Roma at Piazza Antenna (next to the tourist office), Soave ⓣ 045 768 0670

AFTER DARK

These towns are not known for their nightlife, and a night out for locals is more likely to be a convivial evening at a local *trattoria* or a special occasion at one of the more elegant restaurants. For music and dancing the younger set goes to Verona or Lake Garda.

Restaurants
Trattoria da Nicola £ Unfussy local dishes, well prepared. ⓐ Via Valle 41, Monte, Sant'Ambrogio di Valpolicella ⓣ 0457 760 180

Pizzeria Al Castello ££ Excellent pizza and a view of Lake Garda from a hilltop terrace near the Red Cross Monument. ⓐ Piazza Castello, Solferino ⓣ 0376 855 255

Ristorante Lepre ££ Just off the main piazza, Lepre is one of the original restaurants that put Valeggio on the culinary map, and it's still a favourite. Dine in the garden in the summer. ⓐ Via Marsala 5, Valeggio ⓣ 0457 950 011 ⓛ Thur evening–Tues

◖ *Sample the excellent wines of the region*

Ristorante Vittoria ££ A bright dining room serving local specialities, such as pumpkin tortelli and snails with wild greens. ⓐ Via Ossario 37, Solferino ⓣ 0376 854 051

Al Cappello £££ Scallop-filled tortellini put a new spin on the town's speciality. ⓐ Via Antonio Murarri 40, Valeggio ⓣ 045 795 248

Ristorante Arquade £££ The chef insists on the freshest local ingredients, treats them royally and serves them artistically. Dining doesn't get any better, and the service matches the food. If you can splurge on only one meal, book it here. ⓐ Villa Del Quar, Via Quar 12, Pedemonte, Valpolicella ⓣ 045 680 0681 ⓦ www.integra.fr/relaischateaux/delquar

Restaurant d'Amore £££ The location in a hilltop castle and the view would set this restaurant apart, even without the good food and romantic association with the story of the star-crossed lovers. ⓐ Castelli di Romeo e Guilietta, Via Castelli 4 Marteri, Montecchio Maggiore ⓣ 0444 496 6172 ⓛ lunch and dinner Thur–Tues; booking essential.

ACCOMMODATION

Albergo San Giorgio £ The hotel rooms are above a well-patronised family restaurant in this town. ⓐ Via Cavour 12, Valeggio ⓣ 045 795 0125 ⓕ 045 737 0555 ⓦ www.valeggio.com/sangiorgio

Hotel Alla Vittoria £ This classic family-owned *albergo* has stood for almost a century opposite the Museo Storico. Sit on the front

terrace with the locals for a glass of wine in the early evening.
ⓐ Via Ossario 37, Solferino ⓣ/ⓕ 037 685 4051 ⓦ www.darenato.it

Al Gambero ££ Twelve comfortable rooms are inside the walled
town, just through its main gate. It has an excellent restaurant.
ⓐ Corso Vittorio Emanuele 5 ⓣ 045 768 0010 ⓕ 045 619 8301

Roxy Plaza Hotel ££ Right in the centre of town, this large hotel
is near the castle walls that flow downhill through vineyards.
The old town and its *enoteche* are an easy walk from the door.
ⓐ Via San Matteo 4, Soave ⓣ 045 619 0660 ⓕ 045 619 0676
ⓦ www.hotelroxyplaza.it

Il Borghetto £££ You can rent a self-catering apartment in a
renovated water mill dating from 1400, and stay in the little
waterside compound of Borghetto after the toutists have gone
home for the day. ⓐ Villaggio Vacanze Il Borghetto, Via San Raffaello
Sanzio 14A, Valeggio ⓣ 045 795 2040 ⓦ www.borghetto.it

Villa del Quar £££ Staying at this beautifully restored Renaissance
villa is one of life's great pleasures. It is in the midst of the classic
Valpolicella wine region and has an outstanding wine cellar that
includes its own notable wines. The huge outdoor pool is set among
the vineyards. ⓐ Via Quar 12, Pedemonte (Valpolicella region)
ⓣ 045 680 0681 ⓕ 045 680 0604 ⓦ www.hotelvilladelquar.it

Vicenza

Vicenza's claim to immortality is local-boy-made-good, Andrea Palladio. The clean, graceful lines he brought to buildings endure to the 21st century and have inspired buildings all over the world. It is the excellent group of Palladian buildings in the city that earned Vicenza its place as a UNESCO World Heritage Site. Despite its beauty, Vicenza is relatively uncrowded and mellow and is an ideal retreat from the crowds of Verona.

South of Vicenza, the Berici Hills rise suddenly. Scenic roads weave and climb through them, revealing little hilltop villages, castles and some outstanding villas. Some of the best of these are now public buildings, so you can see inside. The towns of Lonigo and Noventa Vicentina are especially worth visiting.

SIGHTS & ATTRACTIONS

A Vicenza Card includes admission to most of the major sights, including Teatro Olimpico and the museums. The Teatro Olimpico admission ticket also admits you to all the museums and is valid for three days, so it might be the more economical choice.

Basilica di Monte Berico

Overlooking the city, the lofty Basilica di Monte Berico was begun in the 15th century in thanksgiving for Vicenza's deliverance from the plague. Now a major pilgrimage site, the ornate interior glows with votive candles. It is home to Montagna's Pietà fresco and an unusual collection of needleworked *ex votos* in a room behind the sanctuary. Veronese's expertly restored *The Supper of Gregory the Great* hangs in the refectory.

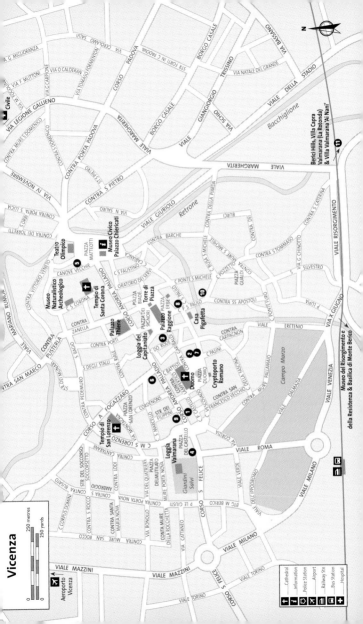

ⓐ Viale X Giugno ❶ 0444 320 998 ⓦ www.monteberico.it
🕐 06.00–12.30, 14.30–18.00 Mon–Sat, 06.00–19.00 Sun; admission free. The first Sunday of each month is a pilgrimage day Ⓝ Bus 18 (Sun only)

Corso Andrea Palladio

Along this backbone of Vicenza are elegant palaces designed by the great names in architecture. The street begins at Piazza Castello, with Palladio's Palazzo Bonin (step into the courtyard to see the interior double loggia). Palazzo Pojana is close to the centre, on the right, easy to recognise by the gate that allows a street to pass through its centre. Palazzo Thiene, on the left, is so large that it has several façades facing onto different streets. At the far end, a fourth palazzo by Palladio is now the civic art museum.

Duomo

The damage of World War II has been so skilfully repaired that the church, founded in the ninth century, doesn't show the scars. The dome, by Palladio (he rarely worked on churches), has been reconstructed, along with the Gothic façade, which is more than a century older.

ⓐ Piazza Duomo 🕐 07.00–12.00, 15.30–19.00; admission free

Giardino Salvi and Loggia Valmarana

Just outside the Porta Castello, with its tower acting as a backdrop to its statuary, is a small park with waterside walkways. Crossing the two branches of a stream are two loggias, one designed by a follower of Palladio and included on the UNESCO list.

▶ *The Palladian masterpiece, Palazzo della Ragione*

Palazzo della Ragione (Basilica Palladiana)

The 15th-century Palazzo della Ragione, better known as the Basilica, is the centrepiece of Vicenza. The soaring loggias that surround the large open interior were built by Palladio in 1549. Attached to it are two towers, the older of which (a medieval prison) overlooks Piazza Erbe.

ⓐ Piazza Signori ⏱ 09.00–17.00 & 10.00–19.00 Tues–Sun (summer); other times for exhibitions. Admission charge for some exhibitions

Piazza dei Signori and Torre di Piazza

A huge statue of Palladio contemplates his work in front of Palazzo della Ragione. Overlooking this beautiful piazza from a greater height is the slender Torre di Piazza, which has grown over the centuries to its present 82 m (269 ft). Opposite, the **Loggia del Capitaniato** is an arcade designed by Palladio. Thursday is market day, when the entire square is filled with stalls.

Teatro Olimpico

The last – and to many the greatest – of Palladio's works remained unfinished when he died, but was completed by his prize student, Vincenzo Scamozzi. Dating from 1589, it is Europe's oldest indoor theatre, designed to feel like a Greek open-air amphitheatre. The stage is a masterpiece of theatrical illusion; it's hard to tell where stage sets end and the painted backdrop begins.

ⓐ Piazza Matteotti ☎ 0444 323 781 ⏱ 09.00–17.00 Tues–Sun; admission charge (ticket includes admission to city-owned museums)

Tempio di San Lorenzo

The Franciscans built the church early in the Middle Ages, and its interior was decorated a few centuries later. Above the front

portal is an especially beautiful and detailed nativity scene.
ⓐ Via Montagna ⓣ 0444 321 960 ⓒ 10.30–12.00 & 15.30–18.00
Mon–Sat, 15.30–18.00 Sun; admission free

Tempio di Santa Corona
The Gothic church was built in the 13th century to house a thorn
from Christ's Crown of Thorns, which you can see annually on
Good Friday. The church contains paintings by Bellini, Veronese
and several others. The church's former convent is now home
to the Museo Naturalistico Archeologico (see Culture,
page 113).
ⓐ Corso Palladio ⓣ 0444 323 644 ⓒ 08.30–12.00, 14.30–18.30;
admission free

Villa Capra Valmarana ('La Rotonda')
Palladio's best-known single work is recognised by Americans as the
model for Thomas Jefferson's home at Montecello.
ⓐ Via della Rotunda (off S-247) ⓣ 0444 321 793 ⓒ grounds
10.00–12.00 & 15.00–18.00 daily (summer); interior 10.00–12.00,
15.00–18.00 Wed ⓝ Bus 8

Villa Valmarana
Often called Villa ai Nani (Villa of the Dwarfs) after the line
of stubby statues that stand atop its wall, Villa Valmarana is
worth seeing for its interior: the rooms are decorated with an
extraordinary cycle of 18th-century frescoes by Tiepolo.
ⓐ Via dei Nani 12 ⓣ 0444 543 976 ⓒ 10.00–12.00, 14.30–17.30
(Mar & Apr), 10.00–12.00, 15.00–18.00 (summer), 10.00–12.00,
14.00–17.00 (Oct & Nov); admission charge ⓝ Bus 8 (walk from
Villa Rotunda)

CULTURE

Museo Civico

Opposite Teatro Olimpico is one of Palladio's grandest city palaces, Palazzo Chiericati, which holds the city's art collection, including works by Bellini, Tiepolo, Montagna and Veronese. Carpione's magnificent frescoed ceiling is near the entrance.

ⓐ Piazza Matteotti ⓣ 0444 321 348 ⓛ 09.00–17.00 Tues–Sun; admission charge (ticket includes Teatro Olimpico and other museums)

◗ *Villa Barbarigo Rezzonico in Noventa Vincentina*

Museo del Risorgimento e della Resistenza

In an art nouveau villa that was headquarters for the Resistance movement, the history of Italy's struggle for independence and unity is shown in an interesting mix of artifacts, photographs and art. Below the museum is a wooded park with walking trails that lead to Villa Rotunda.

ⓐ Vialle X Giugno 115, Monte Berico ☏ 0444 322 998 🕐 09.00–13.00, 14.15–17.00 Tues–Sun. Park 🕐 09.00–19.30 Tues–Sun (summer), 09.00–17.30 Tues–Sun (winter)

Museo Naturalistico Archeologico

The natural life of the Berici hills is explored here, along with prehistoric and ancient finds from the area.

ⓐ Corso Palladio ☏ 0444 320 440 🕐 10.00–18.00 Tues–Sat (July & Aug); 09.00–17.00 Tues–Sat (Sept–June); admission charge (ticket includes Teatro Olimpico and other museums)

RETAIL THERAPY

Vicenza has been a gold capital for centuries, and you'll find small goldsmith's shops tucked under the arcades around Piazza dei Signori and along Corso Andrea Palladio. Thursday is market day, when the entire central city is filled with stalls.

Euro Art Continuing the fine Vicenza art of goldsmithing, this little shop designs and creates elegant jewellery, including tiny gold picture frames to wear. ⓐ Contra San Antonio 9 ☏ 0444 525 222 ⓦ www.euroart.it

Il Ceppo Local food products and wines are on offer in this shop tucked under the portico of Corso Palladio. ⓐ Corso Palladio 196 ① 0444 544 414 ⓦ www.gastronomiailceppo.com

Mercantini Antiquariato From March to December the region's antique dealers hold a large antiques market in the Piazza dei Signori on the second Sunday of the month. ① 044 432 3863

TAKING A BREAK

Antica Bar del Corso £ ❶ The cosy café is under the vaulting, with an airy little outdoor café in a courtyard and good sandwiches. ⓐ Corso Andrea Palladio 54 ① 0444 525 336

Antico Café Scrigni £ ❷ Locals have been sipping espresso and munching cakes here since 1860. ⓐ Piazza Duomo 1 ① 0444 324 920 🕒 closed Mon

Gran Caffè Garibaldi £ ❸ Beside the Loggia del Capitaniato, the raised terrace of the Garibaldi is not only *the* place to be seen, but also provides the best view of the evening *passeggiata*. In bad weather, retreat to the elegant interior. ⓐ Via Cavour 7 (Piazza dei Signori) ① 0444 544 147

Il Torrione Bar Café £ ❹ Under Torre Castello, this tiny wine bar has internet access, excellent wine selection (choose from blackboard) and bruschette. ⓐ Corso Andrea Palladio 3 ① 0444 546 890

▶ *Vicenza is a UNESCO World Heritage Site*

Nirvana Caffe degli Artisti £ ⑤   Cakes and panini (grilled vegetable panini is fresh and delicious) served at tables inside or under the arched portico beside Teatro Olimpico. ⓐ Piazza Matteotti 8 ⓣ 0444 543 111

Zen Zero Café £ ⑥   Spritzers and cocktails with a buffet of food during the aperitivo hours. ⓐ Corso A. Fogazzaro 25 ⓣ 328 392 4925

⬠ *Bargain-hunters search the market stalls*

AFTER DARK

Vicenza has a surprisingly active nightlife for a city of its size, and the tourist office on Piazza dei Signori has a good shelf of flyers on both concert/theatre schedules and the bar/disco scene.

Restaurants

Righetti £ ❼ The only self-service café/restaurant in the city, this friendly local favourite offers snacks from the tiny bar and tasty full meals. ⓐ Piazza Duomo 3 ❶ 0444 543 135

Antica Osteria al Bersagliere £–££ ❽ A few doors downhill from Piazza Erbe, this friendly little place serves excellent meals. ⓐ Corso Pescaria 11 ❶ 0444 323 507 ❷ closed Sun (Note that the city map shows this street as 'Contra P S Paulo'.)

Antica Trattoria Tre Visi ££ ❾ Step through the arched portico of a former palazzo to find this venerable restaurant. ⓐ Corso Andrea Palladio 25 ❶ 0444 324 868 ❷ closed Sun evening; booking advised

Osteria I Monelli ££ ❿ Traditional local dishes served in a warm, inviting rustic atmosphere. It is open later than most restaurants. ⓐ Contra Ponte San Paolo 13 ❶ 0444 540 400 ❷ 10.30–15.00 & 18.30–01.00 Tues–Sun, until 02.00 Fri–Sat

Villa Michelangelo ££–£££ ⓫ The chef is up to the setting – the *agnolotti* are simply the finest on earth. If you don't have a car, the dining experience is well worth the taxi ride from the city centre – or, better yet, stay here overnight (see page 120). ⓐ Via Sacco 35, Arcugnano ❶ 0444 550 300

Cinemas & theatres

Cinemas

Odeon ⓐ Corso Palladio 186 ⓣ 044 454 3492

Patronato Leone III ⓐ C'tra Vittorio Veneto 1 ⓣ 044 432 1457

Primavera (S Bertilla) ⓐ Via F Ozanam 3 ⓣ 044 496 4060

San Marco ⓐ Contra San Francesco 76 ⓣ 044 492 1560

Theatres

Ask at the tourist office for the annual publication *Arte Cultura Spettacoli*, which has complete schedules for all theatres and concert halls.

Teatro Astra A setting for music, drama, opera and jazz; one of the venues for the Vicenza Jazz Festival (see below). ⓐ Contra Barche 53 ⓣ 044 432 3725

Teatro Ca'Balbi A full schedule of touring and locally produced shows, from marionettes to singing groups and comedy theatricals. ⓐ Via Marco Da Montegallo 4 ⓣ 044 491 2779 ⓦ www.teatrocabalbi.com

VICENZA JAZZ

Vicenza has its own Jazz Festival that presents new and less-well-known musicians and singers, as well as a few hot names. Venues are at theatres around the city. Tickets: ⓐ Botteghino del Teatro Olimpico ⓣ call centre 199 112 112 ⓦ www.vivaticket.it. Or from Comune di Vicenza – Assessorato alle Attività Culturali, ⓐ Levà degli Angeli 11 ⓣ 044 422 2122, 422 2116 ⓦ www.comune.vicenza.it

Teatro Olimpico From April to autumn the theatre runs a constant programme of musical productions. ⓐ Botteghino del Teatro Olimpico ⓒ 0444 302 425, box office 199 112 112 ⓦ www.olimpico.vicenza.it

Bars, clubs & discos

Eurodisco One of the most popular places in town, with some well-known DJs spinning on summer weekends. ⓐ Via Commercio 24 ⓒ 044 434 8128

Gio' Music Club Just what it promises: live music, mostly rock and jazz, very popular with locals. ⓐ Via dell'Edilizia 68, Zona Industriale Ovest

Palladium Disco The emphasis is on the music here, with top DJs and a good-sized dance floor. A pizzeria is the newest addition. ⓐ Via G Marconi 119, Torri si Quartesolo ⓒ 0444 583 577 ⓦ www.palladium-italy.com

Victory A classy setting, with live acts and DJs, comfortable tiered table seating and a restaurant. ⓐ Str Biron di Sopra 68/70 ⓒ 044 496 1499 ⓦ www.victoryclub.it

ACCOMMODATION

Camping Vicenza £ A modern campsite in the city, affiliated with the Faita association of campsites. ⓐ Strada Pelosa 239, Vicenza ⓒ 044 458 2311 ⓕ 044 458 2434 ⓦ www.campingvicenza.it

Albergo Acampora ££ On the east side of town and handy for the autostrada, this small, family-run place is comfortable and friendly.

Rooms are air-conditioned and have TV, mini-bars and private phones. Bicycles are available for rent. ⓐ Viale della Pace 32 ⓣ 044 450 4467 ⓕ 044 431 4851 ⓦ www.albergoacampora.it

Hotel Doge ££ This beautifully appointed modern hotel offers secured covered parking, exercise room, satellite TV, PC connections and other amenities. A rooftop patio is a place to relax. Check for web specials. ⓐ Via Lamamora 20 ⓣ 044 492 3616 ⓕ 044 492 8549 ⓦ www.hoteldoge-vi.it

Hotel Giardini ££ Glowing from a complete renovation, the hotel is close to major sights such as the Teatro Olimpico and the Basilica Palladiana. Parking is available. ⓐ Viale Giuriolo 10 ⓣ/ⓕ 044 432 6458 ⓦ www.hotelgiardini.com

Hotel Villa Michelangelo £££ Grace and elegance are the hallmarks of this hilltop villa. The rooms are luxurious without being pompous, and a swimming pool makes this a nice place to escape the summer heat of the valley. Weddings are a speciality, and you couldn't find a more romantic spot. ⓐ Via Sacco 35, Arcugnano ⓣ 044 455 0300 ⓕ 044 455 0490 ⓦ www.hotelvillamichelangelo.com

ⓞ *The attractive piazza at Lonigo, in the province of Vicenza*

Lake Garda

When the summer heat turns the city into a sauna, everyone who can heads to the lake at weekends and in the evening, jostling for space with the Germans who arrive through the Brenner Pass. Beginning at Malcesine, the following destinations are ordered geographically travelling clockwise around the lake.

SIGHTS & ATTRACTIONS

MALCESINE

Most of Garda's towns sit at lake level, but Malcesine's oldest stone buildings cluster around its fortress, on a craggy cliff. From the castle, wander down Via Borre to the Porte Vecchio with its cafés and unique turtle statue, then along Via Capitanato to the boat harbour, where the lake steamers dock. Malcesine is a favourite for tourists, with its steep, narrow streets and abundance of boutiques and restaurants.

Castello Scaligero

This is where Italians held the German writer Goethe prisoner as a spy; now it forms a picturesque backdrop and vantage point for views of the lake. Inside, there is a small museum.

ⓐ Via Borre, Malcesine ⓣ 045 657 0333 ⓛ 09.00–20.00; admission charge

Funivia Panoramica Malcesine-Monte Baldo

Rising 1,600 m (5,250 ft) in about ten minutes, the cable cars turn during the second stage, so all passengers can enjoy the spectacular views. It's a favourite of hikers and mountain bikers,

who can access the higher trails from it (you can rent bikes at the sports shop just below). Bikes and even hang gliders can be taken up for a fee.

ⓐ S-249, Malcesine **ⓣ** 045 740 0206 **ⓦ** www.funiviedelbaldo.it
ⓛ 08.00–18.00

Torri del Bénaco

From this attractive town the lake's only car ferry takes cars back and forth to Maderno on the western shore – a good way to shorten the round-the-lake drive. In the centre of town near the pretty boat harbour, a 13th-century castle houses the **Museo del Castello Scaligero**. The church **Santissima Trinità** has 14th-century frescoes, and nearby Torre di Berengario dates from the 10th century.

Orto Botanica del Monte Baldo

On top of the spine of Monte Baldo, at the end of a long and dizzying road, the high-altitude garden displays native plants, including edelweiss, wild roses and alpine lilies.

ⓐ Ferrara di Monte Baldo (above Garda) **ⓛ** 09.00–18.00 (summer)

BARDOLINO

Bardolino spreads along the shore in what seems like one long piazza, with the water on one side and café umbrellas on the other. Worth seeking out are the 9th-century Carolingian San Zeno and the 11th-century Romanesque San Severo, with a frescoed interior.

ⓞ *Stunning lake views from Gardone Riviera*

LAZISE

The enclosed harbour, which has a Venetian customs station at one side of it, is one of the most picturesque on the lake, with an 11th-century castle, once a Scaligeri stronghold, as a backdrop.

Parco Thermale del Garda

The woods and gardens around the 18th-century Villa Cedri are ideal for strolling and picnicking. There is also a large thermal lake, thermal grotto and a modern spa. Entry to the beautiful park for a day of lounging is good value.

ⓐ Piazza di Sopra 4, Colà di Lazise ⓣ 045 759 0988
ⓦ www.villadeicedri.com

PESCHIERA

One of only two lake towns with train stations, and close to the A4 autostrada, Peschiera is a popular gateway to Lake Garda, and home to its most popular attraction, Gardaland. However, be warned, even in the spring and autumn, the traffic along S11 and S572, the roads closest to the lake, can be bumper-to-bumper at the weekend.

Gardaland

Ride through the land of ships and pirates, explore Africa, dive into the mysteries of Atlantis or enjoy any of the rides at this mother-of-all-theme-parks.

ⓐ S-249, Peschiera ⓣ 045 644 9777 ⓦ www.gardaland.it

SIRMIONE

At the end of a peninsula, this town of narrow, shop-lined streets is almost completely surrounded by water. A medieval castle, Rocca Scaligeri (they were everywhere), still guards the entrance to the town with a narrow drawbridge. No cars are allowed inside (unless you have a hotel reservation there); parking outside the gate fills early in the summer or at weekends. Inside the little moated castle is the Museo del Castello ☎ 030 916 468 ☻ 08.30–13.30 & 15.00–18.00 (summer); 09.00–14.00 Tues–Sun (winter)

Past the shops is the church of **San Pietro in Mavino**, built by the Longobards and rebuilt in 1300, although its campanile dates from 1070. Inside, frescoes from the 12th to the 16th centuries are preserved.

Villa and Grotte di Catullo

Long thought by some to have been the 1st-century BC villa of the poet Catullus, others believe that it must have been a thermal spa. The small antiquarium, a museum at the entrance, contains fragments of recovered fresco.

☎ 030 916 157 ☻ 09.00–dusk Tues–Sun; admission charge

Terme di Sirmione

The thermal waters attracted the Romans to Sirmione and still draw visitors. Since 1884 the waters of a thermal spring have been used for bathing, and modern spas have added other refinements.

☎ 030 990 4923 (freephone in Italy) ☎ 800 802 125
ⓦ www.termedisirmione.com; admission charge

DESENZANO DEL GARDA

Decentius, a Roman nobleman, gave his name to the town and also left behind the ruins of his palatial villa, covered by a mudslide and only unearthed in 1921. Villa Romana has beautiful geometric and figural mosaics, most still in place as they were found.

ⓐ Via Scavi Romani ☎ 030 914 3547 ☻ 09.00–18.30 Tues–Sun (summer); 09.00–17.30 (Mar & Oct); 09.00–16.00 (winter)

SALÒ

Salò sits at the water's edge under the towering Monte San Bartolomeo. In the central lakeside plaza, the arcades of the Loggia della Magnifica Patria are all that remain of the 16th-century Captain's Palace. The 1453 **Duomo**, Santa Maria Annunziata, was never finished outside. The Gothic interior makes up for it. Works by Veronese and several other Italian masters are also in the church. One of the largest of the lake towns, Salò has interesting streets, shops, restaurants and cafés.

GARDONE RIVIERA

Climbing the hillside above Gardone, the André Heller Botanic Garden has exotic plants from all continents, an artificial lake and modern sculptures.

ⓐ Via Roma (S45), Gardone Riviera ⏰ 09.00–19.00 (summer)

Il Vittoriale degli Italiani

The art deco estate was designed for the Italian author, poet, soldier and adventurer Gabriele d'Annunzio. The mansion is stuffed with priceless art and historic objects; the grounds contain a huge mausoleum and a sizeable portion of the warship *Puglia*, alongside other curiosities.

ⓐ Via Vittoriale, Gardone Riviera ☏ 036 520 130 ⏰ 08.00–20.30 (summer); 09.00–12.30, 14.00–17.30 (winter); admission charge for house

MADERNO

North of Gardone Riviera, little Maderno is the town where the cross-lake car ferry docks, connecting to Torri del Bénaco on the

◀ *Lazise's small boat harbour and Venetian customs station*

eastern side. Since earthquakes during 2004 you can't go inside the 12th-century church of Sant Andrea, but stop to see the wonderfully detailed stone carving around the doorway.

CULTURE

Museo Archeologico Rambotti

Roman artefacts and items from the Paleolithic, Mesolithic, Neolithic and Bronze Ages form the collections of this small but very interesting museum.

ⓐ Viale T dal Molin 7c, Desenzano del Garda ❶ 030 914 4529
🕒 15.00–19.00 Tues, Fri–Sun & holidays; admission free

Museo dell'Olio d'Oliva

Olive trees thrive in the temperate climate around the lake, creating an important local industry. This museum tells the story of oil production, and you can sample the results.

ⓐ Via Peschiera 54 (S-249), Cisano di Bardolino
🕒 09.00–12.30 & 14.30–19.00 Mon–Sat, 09.00–12.30 Sun (Mar–Dec)

Museo Del Vino

The Zeni Winery's little museum shows the process by which Garda table wines are produced. There are tastings between mid-March and October, and evening tastings by reservation. ⓐ Via Costabella 9, Bardolino ❶ 045 622 8331 ⓦ www.museodelvino.it 🕒 09.00–13.00 & 14.00–19.00

▶ *Malcesine's fortress tops a craggy cliff*

RETAIL THERAPY

Desenzano and Salò are perhaps the best towns for shopping, but Malcesine has a number of craftsmen's studios and small shops, while Sirmione's streets are lined with the high-end designer and antiquarian shops.

Markets are a regular feature, and you'll find one somewhere nearly every day, though most are filled with cheap imports. Local food producers and craftsmen may have stands at some of them, however. Look for art shows and craft fairs in lake towns, especially at weekends.

Casa Bella Martinelli (Alessi Shop) Take back the latest kitchen gizmo from this classy Lombardy designer. ⓐ Via Pozzo dell'Amore 50, Cavaion Veronese (off the 450 motorway, east of Bardolino) ⓣ 045 626 0344 ⓦ www.casabellamartinelli.it ⓛ 09.00–12.30 & 15.30–19.30 Tues–Sat

Garda Frutta The shop specialises in wines, olive oils and other local foods. ⓐ Via Verona 174, Lugana di Sirmione (opposite Santa Maria church) ⓣ 030 990 5197 ⓦ www.martellifood.it ⓛ 08.30–13.00 & 16.00–20.00 Tues–Sun (summer); 08.30–12.30 & 16.00–19.30 Tues–Sat (winter)

Marisa Castellini Quadri-Miniature Local artists of some note – not to mention talent – are represented here, at affordable prices. ⓐ Via Lungolago D'Annunzio 22, Gardone Riviera ⓣ 0365 290 236

◀ *The attractive harbour at Desenzano*

Soul Light Original, stylish candles in vivid colours, for every occasion. ⓐ Via Castello 23, Desenzano ⓣ 030 991 1514 ⓦ www.soullight.it ⓛ 15.30–20.00 Mon–Tues, Thur–Fri, 09.30–13.00, 15.00–20.00 Sat–Sun

TAKING A BREAK

You won't want for places to sit along the lake and enjoy a *prosecco* or cappuccino, since every town's waterfront is lined with café umbrellas.

Bar Al Porto £ The best-located café tables in Lazise, right on the corner of the lake-shore promenade and the charming boat harbour, at the point where the NaviGarda lake steamers dock. ⓐ Lungolago Marconi 2, Lazise ⓣ 045 758 0538

Bar Pasticceria Bosio £ Not only the oldest, but the best pastry café in town, this one specialises in traditional local cakes. ⓐ Piazza Malvezzi 5, Desenzano del Garda ⓣ 030 914 2330

Caracas Pub £ 'The baddest pub on Lake Garda' is how its sign translates, and at night the place rocks. By day the garden terrace is a good place for lunch. ⓐ Via Carere 2, Gardone Sopra

Pizzeria La Strambata £ Leave the crowded lake shore to join locals for pizza or enormous *salade caprese*. Via Fosse, Bardolino ⓣ 045 721 0110.

⓿ *Al-fresco dining in Malcesine*

AFTER DARK

The liveliest towns for nightlife tend to be on the southern and eastern shores: Desenzano, Garda, Bardolino and Lazise. Look to Salò, Gardone Riviera and Sirmione for more high-class entertainment aimed at a slightly older age group.

Restaurants

Bar Ristorante La Taverna £–££ Family-run and very friendly, this little taverna serves delicious gnocchi. ⓐ Via Del Republic 343, Gardone Riviera ⓣ 036 520 412 ⓛ closed Tues

Osteria alla Rosa £–££ All the pasta is made right on the premises, or try the polenta with sausages or fresh fish from the lake. ⓐ Piazza Bocchera 5 (Via Cerche), Malcesine ⓣ 045 657 0783

Trattoria La Biocca ££ The *ravioli di zucca al burro e salvia* (pumpkin ravioli with butter and sage) are excellent, but you can't go wrong with anything you order here. ⓐ Vicolo Molino 6 ⓣ 0309 143 658 ⓛ closed Thur

Agli Angeli ££–£££ Go here for an exceptional dinner, with professional (but friendly) service and artistically presented dishes. ⓐ Via Cadute 1, Gardone Sopra ⓣ 0365 20 832 ⓛ closed Mon (and Wed mid-Oct–mid-Mar)

Villa del Sogno £££ Dinner is a class act, with creative takes on local products, artful presentation and polished, friendly service. ⓐ Via Zanardelli 107, Gardone Riviera ⓣ 0365 290 181 ⓦ www.villadelsogno.it

Cinemas & theatre
Cinema Casino ⓐ Via Zanardelli 142, Gardone Riviera ⓣ 0365 218 81
Cinema Teatro Alberti ⓐ Via Santa Maria, Desenzano ⓣ 030 914 1513
Cinema Teatro Cristal ⓐ Largo del' Alighieri, Salò ⓣ 0365 521 555

Bars & clubs
Café Bar Taverna This lively (make that raucous, at night) spot is a perennial fave for a glass of wine and often live music. ⓐ Piazza Catullo, Garda

Euroclub 80 The flashiest place in town, on the hill behind Villa Alba. ⓐ Via Vittoriale 11, Gardone Riviera ⓣ 0365 223 36

Taverna Fregoso You can have dinner or pizza here, but most go for the wine and the live music every night (21.00–02.00) in the summer. ⓐ Corso Vittore Emanuele 39, Garda ⓣ 0457 256 622 ⓛ closed Wed

ACCOMMODATION

Hotel Garni Diana £–££ All rooms in this hotel have balconies with views of the lake or Monte Baldo. Outdoor swimming pool. ⓐ Via Scoisse 8, Malcesine ⓣ 045 750 0192 ⓕ 045 740 0415 ⓦ www.dianamalcesine.com

Hotel Roma £–££ All rooms in the newly renovated hotel have terraces or balconies on the lake front. Parking available. ⓐ Lungolago Regina Adelaide 8, Garda ⓣ 045 725 5025 ⓕ 045 627 0266 ⓦ www.hotelromagarda.it ⓛ Mar–Oct

Hotel Vittorio ££ A beautiful example of Italian art deco on the lake shore. Almost every room has a lake or harbour view: ask for corner room 410 for the best of both. ⓐ Via Porto Vecchio 4, Descenzano ⓣ 030 991 2245 ⓕ 030 991 2270 ⓦ www.hotelvittorio.it

Villa Del Sogno £££ On the hillside overlooking the lake, gardens surround the art deco building, whose central terrace is like a small private piazza. ⓐ Via Zanardelli 107, Gardone Riviera ⓣ 036 529 0181 ⓕ 036 529 0230 ⓦ www.villadelsogno.it

Camping
Camping Cappuccini Tent and caravan pitches with showers, shelters, swimming, beaches. ⓐ Località Cappuccini, Peschiera del Garda ⓣ 045 755 1592 ⓕ 045 755 1592 ⓦ www.camp-cappuccini.com ⓛ Mar–Sept

Camping Cisano A large camping area with shelters, and bungalows also available. The complex includes a supermarket, restaurant, whirlpool and more. ⓐ Via Peschiera 48, Frazione Cisano, Bardolino ⓣ/ⓕ 045 622 9059 ⓦ www.camping-cisano.it

● *One of Villa Valmarana's dwarf statues*

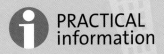

Directory

GETTING THERE

By air

From the UK and Europe Several European airlines fly into Verona's Catullo airport (☎ 04 809 5666) in Villafranca, about 16 km (9½ miles) southwest of the centre. Low-cost Ryanair (ⓦ www.ryanair.com) flies from London's Stansted airport to Aeroporto Brescia ☎ 030 965 6502 ⓦ www.bresciaairport.com, just west of Lake Garda.

Milan's Malpensa airport is northern Italy's major air hub for those arriving from outside Europe. Verona is a 90-minute train ride from Milan's Stazione Centrale, which is easily reached from the airport via a paying shuttle bus that waits directly outside the arrival gate.

From North America there are direct flights from the USA and Canada gateways to Milan's Malpensa airport via Alitalia (ⓦ www.alitalia.com), Continental (ⓦ www.continental.com) and several other airlines. It is possible to connect with onward flights to Verona, but the cost is often not worth the short time saved over getting there by train from Milan.

You can sometimes combine airfare, lodging and car hire into a money-saving package. Ask about the possibilities when booking flights. It is wise to secure your trip with travel insurance.

Many people are aware that air travel emits CO_2, which contributes to climate change. You may be interested in the possibility of lessening the environmental impact of your flight through the charity Climate Care, which offsets your CO_2 by funding environmental projects around the world. Visit www.climatecare.org

⏵ *Cruising on Lake Garda*

By train

With the arrival of the Eurostar, Milan's Stazione Centrale is on a direct rail link with Geneva, making the trip from London's Waterloo Station to Milan about 12 hours, with onward connections to Verona adding 90 minutes to the trip. Less pricey are conventional trains. Verona is also on the main line from Paris to Venice. Travel time is about 5 hours to Milan from Paris by Eurostar, 7 hours by slower train. Italian trains run on time (Ⓦ www. trenitalia.it). Be sure to have your ticket date-stamped in one of the machines on the platform of the station before boarding.

Travellers from outside Europe who plan to use trains should investigate the various multiday train passes on Trenitalia and multi country travel offered by Rail Europe (Ⓦ www.raileurope.com). For travellers anywhere, Rail Europe offers a one-stop source of information, reservations and tickets, including Eurostar.

By bus

Barring a very cheap flight, the cheapest way to Verona from the UK is by bus, about 26 hours from London's Victoria Coach Station via Eurolines UK (❶ 08705 143219 Ⓦ www.gobycoach.com or Ⓦ www.eurolines.com).

By car

The Mont Blanc Tunnel takes you through the Alps to Verona, Milan, along the A5 and A4 autostrada. In Italy, as in the rest of the continent, driving is on the right-hand side of the road.

ENTRY FORMALITIES

Citizens of Ireland, USA, Canada, New Zealand, Australia, Singapore and Israel need only a valid passport to enter Italy and do not require visas for stays of up to 90 days. UK citizens may stay without a visa for an unlimited period. Citizens of South Africa must have visas to enter Italy.

EU citizens can bring goods for personal use when arriving from another EU country, but must observe the limits on tobacco (800 cigarettes) and spirits (10 litres over 22 per cent alcohol, 90 litres of wine). Limits for non-EU nationals are 200 cigarettes, one litre of spirits and two litres of wine.

MONEY

The euro (€) is the official currency in Italy. Currency exchange facilities and ATMs are near the arrival gates at Malpensa, Catullo and Brescia airports. An ATM is in the rail station in Verona, but it is wise to arrive with some euros, especially at the weekend.

Avoid carrying large amounts of cash and, if you must, hide it well in several concealed pockets and security pouches. Safer are traveller's cheques, accepted at banks, large hotels and by larger stores, but difficult to cash elsewhere. If possible, bring at least one major credit card: Visa is the most commonly accepted. Many small hotels, *agriturismo* properties and small restaurants do not accept cards. Expect trouble trying to cash eurocheques except in large banks.

Best for obtaining euros are credit or debit cards. ATMs (*bancomat*) offer the best exchange rates and are found even in small towns. Ask your card issuer before leaving home what network you can use in Italy and make sure that your PIN number can be used abroad. Banks are usually open 08.30–13.00 or 13.30 Mon–Fri. Try to have enough euros to last over weekends, when banks close and ATMs may be out of money or out of order.

HEALTH, SAFETY & CRIME

Verona is considered a safe city, but in any large city you need to be aware of your surroundings, and avoid walking alone at night or in places that are not well lit. Guard against pickpockets by carrying (well hidden) only the cash you need. Waist packs and bum bags label you as a tourist and make you a particular target anywhere. Be especially wary of crowded areas, such as train stations, buses and street markets. Avoid groups of small children who try to engage you in conversation; they are fast and work expertly in teams. Keep cameras firmly in your hand and the strap around your neck. As anywhere, don't leave cameras or handbags slung over the back of your chair in a restaurant.

Report any thefts immediately, and be sure to get a copy of the police report (*denuncia*) for insurance. Police are of two varieties: the *carabinieri* (national police), and the *vigili* (local officers). Both are armed and can make arrests, but the *vigili* are usually more concerned with traffic and parking. Police normally wear white uniforms in the summer, black in the winter. You can report a crime to either, but the paperwork must be completed at a *questura* (police station).

Drinking water is safe in Verona, Vicenza and around Lake Garda, as is the food; it is wise to carry your favourite medication for an upset stomach, since travellers anywhere are more likely to eat and drink things their systems are unaccustomed to. Should you become ill or have an accident, medical care is quite good and free to EU residents. The E111 form is no longer valid. You will need a European Health Insurance Card (EHIC) to receive healthcare during a visit to a EU country or Switzerland. Non-EU residents should carry travellers' health insurance if their own coverage does not cover reimbursement, and should also consider emergency medical evacuation insurance. Emergency treatment at hospitals is free to

everyone. For police and medical emergency numbers, see
Emergencies, page 154.

As a pedestrian, always look both ways when crossing, even on
one-way streets, since bus lanes sometimes travel in the opposite
direction. Those from left-hand drive countries need to be especially
careful because traffic will be approaching from an unexpected
direction. Scooters and motorbikes are common, and you should
always be aware of these approaching between vehicles or
emerging suddenly from alleyways.

OPENING HOURS
Most of Verona's major attractions open 08.30 or 09.00–19.00 or
19.30 with Monday morning closing. Smaller ones and some
churches may have shorter hours, frequently closing for lunch.
The major churches are open through the day, without lunchtime
closing from March to October. Hours are subject to change, so ask
at the tourist office for the most up-to-date times (websites are
notoriously out of date). Banks open 08.30–13.00 or 13.30 Mon–Fri.
Larger stores generally open 09.00 or 10.00–19.00 or 19.30 Mon–Sat,
smaller ones usually close from 12.30 until 15.30 in the summer, with
a shorter midday closing in the winter and Monday morning closing.
Sunday afternoon openings are becoming more common. Food
shops close on Wednesday afternoons. Street markets open about
07.00 and close around midday. Chemists (pharmacies) are usually
open 08.00–13.00 and 16.00–20.00 Mon–Sat, and a sign
on the door will direct you to the nearest one open longer hours.

TOILETS
Public buildings, such as museums, usually have clean toilets in the
publicly accessible areas near the entrance (or will let you in to use

one if you look desperate), and you will find public facilities at Piazza Brà (enter from the park, just opposite the Pallazo della Gran Guardia) and near the church of San Zeno. The easiest solution elsewhere is to step into a bar or café and go directly to the back, following the sign 'toilet' or the universal symbols. Buying a drink is polite. Some of these may not be the cleanest you have ever encountered (always carry your own paper), but they are available. At public toilets, be prepared to pay a small fee, usually €0.50.

CHILDREN

Italians love children and it is becoming more and more common to see them in restaurants, even in the evening – although it's rare in upmarket restaurants. Better to choose a small *trattoria*, where your whole family will be welcomed. Hotels can usually provide cots with advance notice, and you will rarely be charged for a child staying in a room with adults. Special infant needs, such as baby food and nappies, are available in supermarkets (PAM supermarket is just off Piazza Brà), but for a shorter stay it is easier to bring familiar brands from home.

The most child-friendly sights in Verona are those left by the Romans: the **Arena**, **Teatro Romano** and the **Arco dei Gavi** (be sure they find the chariot tracks in the stones underneath this one). Kids also like the castellated bridge at **Castelvecchio** (there is a play park for them at the far end) and the natural history museum, where there are lots of fossils. **Giardino Guisti** has a hedge maze that is fun even for young children, since they can see over the top. Also, be sure they try to find the hollow spots on the statue as they enter the garden; a mallet is hanging there handily for this experiment. When energy flags, head for one of Verona's many *gelato* (ice-cream) counters – there is an especially good one just outside the gate at the end of Piazza Brà.

Lake Garda, the Valpolicella region and other towns close to Verona hold a number of attractions that kids will like, including the obvious theme parks and water amusements, such as the almost overwhelming **Gardaland**. Castles are always good, and you'll find these in Sirmione, Malchesine and Soave. Malcesine also has a revolving cable car to the mountaintop of **Monte Baldo**. Boat rides on the lake are a diversion, too.

In the lake towns, look for kiddie playgrounds, with slides and climbing jungles, swings and other toys. In Verona you'll find one at the other side of Ponte Scaligeri. Each May, Verona has the Mondadori Junior Festival, where at weekends kids can learn to make ravioli, meet story-book characters, play on rides and take part in a city-full of other activities. Festivals of any kind always have children's activities and are colourful, lively occasions with music.

COMMUNICATIONS

Phone

All Verona numbers begin with 045. Numbers vary between eight and nine digits, with a few shorter ones remaining. Numbers beginning with 800 are free. To use public telephones, buy a card (*carta telefonica*) from a *tabaccherie*. Hotel telephones usually carry a high surcharge; check at the desk.

To make an international call, dial 00, then the country code (UK = 44, Ireland = 353, US and Canada = 1, Australia = 61, New Zealand = 64) and number, omitting the initial zero in UK numbers. To call Verona from outside Italy, dial the international access code (00 in the UK and Ireland, 011 in the US), then Italy's country code of 39, then the number beginning with 045.

Mobile phone numbers begin with 3; if you see an old number with the prefix 03, omit the zero. Your UK, New Zealand and

Australian mobile phone will work in Italy; US and Canadian cellphones will not. Travellers from those countries can solve this easily with a universal mobile from Mobal, a UK firm with cutting-edge expertise in international communications. These mobiles work anywhere in the world, with a permanent UK number that travels with you (UK ❶ 1543 426 999 ❶ 1543 426 126 Ⓦ www.mobell.co.uk; US ❶ 888 888 9162 (free call) or 212 785 5800 Ⓦ www.mobalrental.com).

Post and internet
The Italian postal service is quite reliable. For letters and postcards you can buy stamps at a tobacconist's, and for special services you can go to a post office (Central Post Office at Piazza Viviani or Via Carlo Cattaneo) ❶ 045 800 3998 Ⓦ www.posteitaliane.it

Internet is increasingly available, both in hotels and at internet points and cafés around the city. Tourist information offices and kiosks can provide lists of internet cafés and public access points such as libraries. ❶ Picture ID is now required to use the internet under Italy's anti-terrorism legislation.

ELECTRICITY
Electrical appliances used in the UK will work in Italy, but those from the US and Canada will need an adapter to convert from 110v to 220v. Travellers from the UK and elsewhere will also need adapters, as Italian sockets are for plugs with two round pins.

TRAVELLERS WITH DISABILITIES
Airport Assistance: A programme called the Sala Amica provides assistance on check-in, boarding and disembarkation at both of Milan's major airports. Wheelchairs are carried free. Check-in is at

the Sala Amica. Make arrangements to be met when booking your flight. ⓐ Malpensa Terminal 1 ✆ 02 5858 0298 ⓐ Malpensa Terminal 2 ✆ 02 5858 3266 ⓐ Linate ✆ 02 716 659. When travelling to Brescia or Verona Catullo, check with your airline about facilities and help for the disabled.

Access to trains: Look for the booklet *I Servizi per la Clientela Disabile* at any rail station, listing the stations with disabled reception centres (Centro di Accoglienza Disabili). For assistance at **Stazione Centrale** in Milan, call ✆ 02 6707 0958. The ticket station and the waiting areas are accessible and the platforms are accessed by lift. All tracks at Verona's rail station have lift access, but special assistance is required for boarding trains at any station. Be sure to allow extra time.

TOURIST INFORMATION

UPT ⓐ Via Alpini 11, off Piazza Brà ✆ 045 806 8680 🖷 45 800 3638 ⓦ www.tourism.verona.it 🕐 daily; weekdays only in winter. Expect long queues here in the summer.

UPT ⓐ Railway Station, Porta Nuova ✆ 045 800 0861 🕐 daily, all year round, but with limited information

Turismo ⓐ Ponte Aleardi at Via Pallone and Via Macello 🕐 09.00–18.00 Mon–Fri, 09.00–12.30 & 14.00–17.30 Sat & Sun. No telephone enquiries.

Useful websites

For good, current information on the city, visit
Ⓦ http://portale.comune.verona.it and Ⓦ www.italiantourism.com,
the Italian national tourism (Ente Nazionale Italiano per il Turismo,
or ENIT) site, which has general information on travel in Italy, as well
as regional coverage.

Italian overseas tourist offices

Italian State Tourist Office ⓐ 1 Princes Street, London W1R 8AY,
England Ⓣ 020 7408 1254 Ⓦ www.enit.it

Italian Government Tourist Board ⓐ 630 Fifth Ave, Suite 1565, New
York, NY 10111, USA Ⓣ 212 245 5618

Italian Government Tourist Board ⓐ 175 Bloor Street East, Suite 907
– South Tower, Toronto, ON M4W 3R8, Canada Ⓣ 416 925 4882
Brochures Ⓣ 416 925 3870

Italian Government Tourist Office ⓐ 44 Market St, Level 6, Sydney
NSW 2000, Australia Ⓣ 02 9262 1666 Ⓦ www.italiantourism.com.au

Italian Tourist Office, Italian Embassy ⓐ 796 George Avenue, Arcadia
0083, Pretoria, South Africa Ⓣ 012 430 5541

Italian Tourist Office, Italian Embassy ⓐ 34–38 Grant Road,
Thorndon, Wellington, New Zealand Ⓣ 04 4947 173

Ⓞ *Monte Baldo cable car*

Useful phrases

Although English is spoken in many tourist locations in Verona, these words and phrases may come in handy. See also the phrases for specific situations in other parts of this book.

English	Italian	Approx. pronunciation
BASICS		
Yes	Sì	See
No	No	Noh
Please	Per favore	Perr fahvawreh
Thank you	Grazie	Grahtsyeh
Hello	Salve	Sahlveh
Goodbye	Arrivederci	Arreevehderrchee
Excuse me	Scusi	Skoozee
Sorry	Scusi	Skoozee
That's okay	Va bene	Vah behneh
To	A	Ah
From	Da	Dah
I don't speak Italian	Non parlo italiano	Nawn parrlaw itahlyahnaw
Do you speak English?	Parla inglese?	Parrla eenglehzeh?
Good morning	Buon giorno	Booawn geeyawrnaw
Good afternoon	Buon pomeriggio	Booawn pawmehreehdjaw
Good evening	Buonasera	Booawnah sehrah
Goodnight	Buonanotte	Booawnah nawtteh
My name is ...	Mi chiamo ...	Mee kyahmaw ...
DAYS & TIMES		
Monday	Lunedì	Loonehdee
Tuesday	Martedì	Marrtehdee
Wednesday	Mercoledì	Merrcawlehdee
Thursday	Giovedì	Jawvehdee
Friday	Venerdì	Venerrdee
Saturday	Sabato	Sahbahtaw
Sunday	Domenica	Dawmehneeca
Morning	Mattino	Mahtteenaw
Afternoon	Pomeriggio	Pawmehreedjaw
Evening	Sera	Sehra
Night	Notte	Notteh
Yesterday	Ieri	Yeree

English	Italian	Approx. pronunciation
Today	Oggi	Odjee
Tomorrow	Domani	Dawmahnee
What time is it?	Che ore sono?	Keh awreh sawnaw?
It is ...	Sono le ...	Sawnaw leh ...
09.00	Nove	Noveh
Midday	Mezzogiorno	Metsawjorrnaw
Midnight	Mezzanotte	Metsanotteh

NUMBERS

One	Uno	Oonaw
Two	Due	Dweh
Three	Tre	Treh
Four	Quattro	Kwahttraw
Five	Cinque	Cheenkweh
Six	Sei	Say
Seven	Sette	Setteh
Eight	Otto	Ottaw
Nine	Nove	Noveh
Ten	Dieci	Dyehchee
Eleven	Undici	Oondeechee
Twelve	Dodici	Dawdeechee
Twenty	Venti	Ventee
Fifty	Cinquanta	Cheenkwahnta
One hundred	Cento	Chentaw

MONEY

I would like to change these traveller's cheques/this currency	Vorrei cambiare questi assegni turistici/ questa valuta	Vawrray cahmbyahreh kwestee assenee tooree- steechee/kwesta vahloota
Where is the nearest ATM?	Dov'è il bancomat più vicino?	Dawveh eel bankomaht pyoo veecheenaw?
Do you accept credit cards?	Accettate carte di credito?	Achetahteh kahrrteh dee krehdeehtaw?

SIGNS & NOTICES

Airport	Aeroporto	Ahaerrhawpawrrtaw
Railway station	Stazione ferroviaria	Stahtsyawneh ferrawvyarya
Platform	Binario	Binahriaw
Smoking/ non-smoking	Per fumatori/ non fumatori	Perr foomahtawree/ non foomahtawree
Toilets	Gabinetti	Gabinetteh
Ladies/Gentlemen	Signore/Signori	Seenyawreh/Seenyawree
Subway	Metropolitana	Metrawpawleetahna

Emergencies

POLICE

Should you need to report a theft (*furto*), missing person or any other matter to the police, go to the *questura* (police station). If insurance is involved, ask for a *denuncia*, a stamped form that you must have for filing claims.

Questura (Main Police Station) ⓐ Lungadige Galtarossa ⓣ 045 809 0411, foreign section ⓣ 045 809 0500

Polizia Municipale (City Police) ⓐ Via dedel Pontiere 32A ⓣ 045 807 8411

To reach the police in an emergency, dial:
112 for Carabinieri or
113 for local police.

To report a fire, dial **115**.

EMERGENCY PHRASES

Help! Aiuto! *Ahyootaw!*   **Fire!** Al fuoco! *Ahl fooawcaw!*
Stop! Ferma! *Fairmah!*

Call an ambulance/a doctor/the police/the fire service!
Chiamate un'ambulanza/un medico/la polizia/i pompieri!
Kyahmahteh oon ahmboolahntsa/oon mehdeecaw/la pawleetsya/ee pompee-ehree!

LOST PROPERTY

Oggetti Smarriti Via campo Marzo 9 045 807 9341

MEDICAL

Should you become ill while travelling, you have several sources of information on English-speaking doctors. If you can reach your consulate, it can provide a list, or you can go prepared with the appropriate pages from the directory published by IAMAT. The International Association of Medical Assistance for Travellers is a non-profit organisation that provides medical information on health-related travel issues all over the world, as well as a list of English-speaking doctors (www.iamat.org). Hospital accident and emergency departments (ask for the *pronto soccorso*) are open 24 hours daily and must treat you free of charge in an emergency.

Medical Emergency Dial **118**, a free call to ambulances and emergency medical care.

Chemists (Pharmacies) Emergency Information 045 801 1148 www.farmacieverona.it

AUTOMOBILE

Members of the Automobile Association in the UK have reciprocal privileges with the Italian Automobile Association. For roadside assistance and breakdowns, contact ACI Breakdown Service 116

CONSULATES & EMBASSIES

In general, it is a consulate that handles emergencies of travelling citizens, not the embassy. But if there is no consulate in a country, then embassies take over these responsibilities. Your nearest consulate or embassy should be the first place you turn to if a passport is lost, after reporting it to the police. Consulates can also provide lists of English-speaking doctors and dentists and find you an English-speaking lawyer.

British Consulate General ⓐ Via S Paolo 7, 20121 Milano ⓣ 02 723 001, after office hours 335 810 6857 ⓕ 02 864 65081 ⓦ www.britishembassy.gov.uk/italy

American Consulate General ⓐ Via Principe Amedeo 2, 20121 Milano ⓣ 02 626 88520 ⓕ 02 659 6561 ⓦ www.usembassy.it

Australian Consulate General ⓐ 3rd Floor, Via Borgogna 2, 20122 Milano ⓣ 02 777 041 ⓕ 02 777 04242 ⓦ www.australian-embassy.it

New Zealand Embassy ⓐ Via Zara 28, 00198 Roma ⓣ 06 441 7171 ⓕ 06 440 2984

South African Consul General ⓐ Vicolo S Giovanni sul Muro 4, 20121 Milano ⓣ 02 885 8581 ⓦ www.sudafrica.it

Embassy of Canada, Consular Section ⓐ Via Zara 30, 00198 Roma ⓣ 06 445 981, automated information line 06 445 983 937 ⓕ 06 445 983 750

▶ *Ice cream is an Italian speciality*

INDEX

A

accommodation 32–37, 104–105, 119–120, 137–138
air travel 140
airports 46, 140
Arche Scaligeri 56
Arco dei Gavi 78
Arena 12–13, 78, 80
Arena & West 50, 78
arts see culture

B

Bardolino 125
bars & clubs 29, 76–77, 91–92, 119, 137
Basilica di Monte Berico 106, 108
Basilica Palladiana 108, 110
Berici Hills 106
Borghetto 96–97
bridges 63–64, 99
bus travel 47, 50–51

C

cafés 24–25, 72, 87, 100, 103, 114, 116, 134
camping 36, 138
Cangrande statue 44–45
car hire 54
Carnevale di Verona 8
Casa di Giulietta 59
Castel San Pietro 59
Castello Scaligero 122
Castelvecchio 44–45, 80, 84–85
children 146–147
cinema 91, 118
coach travel 142
consulates 155–156
Corso Andrea Palladio 108
Corso Cavour Palazzi 80–81
crime 47, 50, 144

culture 8–13, 18–20, 29, 44–45, 64–65, 66, 68–69, 81, 82–83, 84–86, 99–100, 111–113, 118–119, 130
customs & duty 143

D

dance 20
Desenzano del Garda 127
disabilities, travellers with 148–149
driving 47, 142, 145, 155
Duomo (Salò) 129
Duomo (Verona) 59–60
Duomo (Vicenza) 108

E

electricity 148
embassies 155–156
emergencies 144–145, 154–155
entertainment 12–13, 20, 28–29 see also nightlife
environs of Verona 94
events 8–13

F

fashion 22, 69, 70, 71, 86–87
festivals 8, 9–10, 11–13
food & drink 9–10, 11, 24–27, 70, 96, 98, 99, 130
frescoes 83, 84, 85
Funivia Panoramica Malcesine-Monte Baldo 122, 125

G

Gardaland 126
Gardone Riviera 129
gates 42–43, 65, 78
Giardino Giusti 60
Giardino Salvi 108
goldsmithing 113

H

health 144–145, 155

history 14–15, 96
hostels 36
hotels 32–37, 104–105, 120, 137–138

I

Il Vittoriale degli Italiani 129
insurance 144
internet 32–33, 148

L

Lake Garda 20, 23, 122
language 23, 27, 51, 152–153, 154
Lazise 126
lifestyle 6, 16, 47
Loggia Valmarana 108

M

Maderno 129–130
Malcesine 122
markets 23, 63, 133
Molina Parco delle Cascate 98
money 27, 143
Montecchio Maggiore 94
Museo degli Affreschi 85
Museo Archeologico 68
Museo Archeologico Rambotti 130
Museo Castelvecchio 44, 80, 84–85
Museo Civico 112
Museo Civico di Storia Naturale 85
Museo Lapidario Maffeiano 86
Museo Miniscalchi-Erizzo 68–69
Museo Naturalistico Archeologico 113
Museo dell'Olio d'Oliva 130
Museo Preistorico e Paleontologico 99

Museo del Risorgimento e della Resistenza 113
Museo Storico 99–100
Museo del Vino 130
music 12–13, 20, 29, 76, 90–92, 118–119, 137

N
nightlife 12–13, 20, 28–29, 73–77, 88–92, 103–104, 117–119, 136–137

O
Old Centre 50, 56
opening hours 26–27, 143, 145
opera 12–13, 19
Orto Botanica del Monte Baldo 125

P
Palazzo Forti Galleria d'Arte Moderna 69
Palladio, Andrea 106, 108, 109–110
Parco Thermale del Garda 126
passports & visas 142–143
Peschiera 126
phones 147–148
Piazza Brà 81
Piazza Erbe 63
Piazza dei Signori (Verona) 60, 63
Piazza dei Signori (Vicenza) 110
Pojega 98
police 144, 154
Ponte Pietra 63–64
Ponte Scaligero 80
Ponte di Veja 99
post 148
prehistoric remains 99
public holidays 11
public transport 46, 50–53, 142

R
rail station 46, 50–51
rail travel 142
restaurants 25–27, 72–73, 74–75, 88–90, 103–104, 117, 134–135, 136
Romeo & Juliet 58, 94

S
safety 47, 50, 144, 145
Salò 129
San Fermo 81–82
San Giorgio 98
San Lorenzo 82
San Pietro in Mavino 127
San Zeno in Oratorio 82–83
Sanmicheli, Michele 42–43
Sant'Anastasia 64
Santa Maria Antica 64
Santa Maria in Organo 64–65
Scala, della (family) 14, 44–45, 56, 64
Scarpa, Carlo 44–45
Scavi Archeologici 65
seasons 8
Shakespeare, William 6, 61
shopping 22–23, 63, 69–71, 86–87, 100, 113–114, 133–134
Sirmione 126–127
Soave 94, 96
Solferino 96
spas 31, 127
sport 30–31

T
taxis 54
Teatro Olimpico 110
Teatro Romano 66
Tempio di San Lorenzo 110–111
Tempio di Santa Corona 111

Terme di Sirmione 31, 127
theatre 118–119
time differences 46
tipping 27
toilets 145–146
Tomba di Giulietta 66
Torre Lamberti 66, 68
Torre di Piazza 110
Torri del Bénaco 125
tourist information 149–150

V
Valeggio 96–97
Valpolicella 98–99
Vicenza 106
Villa & Grotte di Catullo 127
Villa Capra Valmarana 111
Villa Cedri 126
Villa Valmarana 111

W
walls 42, 83–84
weather 8, 44–45
wine 10, 11, 26, 98, 99

The publishers would like to thank the following for supplying the copyright photos for this book: Pictures Colour Library pages 1, 55; all the rest Stillman Rogers.

Copy editor: Penny Isaac
Proofreader: Emma Sangster

Send your thoughts to
books@thomascook.com

- **Found a great bar, club, shop or must-see sight that we don't feature?**

- **Like to tip us off about any information that needs updating?**

- **Want to tell us what you love about this handy little guidebook and more importantly how we can make it even handier?**

Then here's your chance to tell all! Send us ideas, discoveries and recommendations today and then look out for your valuable input in the next edition of this title. As an extra 'thank you' from Thomas Cook Publishing, you'll be automatically entered into our exciting monthly prize draw.

Send an email to the above address (stating the book's title) or write to:
CitySpots Project Editor, Thomas Cook Publishing, PO Box 227,
The Thomas Cook Business Park, Unit 18, Coningsby Road,
Peterborough PE3 8SB, UK.